OUTGROWING
THE INGROWN
CHURCH

OUTGROWING THE INGROWN CHURCH

C. John Miller

Foreword by Frank R. Tillapaugh

Ministry Resources Library

Zondervan Publishing House • Grand Rapids, MI

Outgrowing the Ingrown Church
Copyright © 1986 by C. John Miller

Ministry Resources Library is an imprint of Zondervan Publishing House,
1415 Lake Drive, S.E., Grand Rapids, Michigan 49506.

Library of Congress Cataloging in Publication Data

Miller, C. John.
   Outgrowing the ingrown church.

   Includes bibliographies.
   1. Church renewal. 2. Mission of the church. I. Title.
BV600.2.M529   1986   266   86-14170
ISBN 0-310-28411-2

The real names of my family members and leaders at New Life Church are
used in this book. In the other instances, secondary details have been altered
to prevent identification of individuals and churches.

Edited by Susan Lutz and James E. Ruark
Designed by Louise Bauer

Printed in the United States of America

        87   88   89   90   91 / 10   9   8   7   6   5   4   3   2

To Ron Lutz,

my faithful friend,
co-laborer and fellow pastor,
and wise pacesetter for Christ at New Life Church

CONTENTS

FOREWORD

As we knock on the door of the twenty-first century, we must deal with the Ingrown Church. Evangelical strength today is found in paraministries, schools, and publishing houses, but it is not in the ministry effectiveness of the vast majority of local churches.

The reason for that lack of ministry effectiveness, John Miller says, is that our churches have become self-centered and ingrown. His objective is not to see small ingrown churches become large ingrown churches. Instead, his burden is primarily a burden for the kingdom of God and not for any particular local church. His emphasis is on the basic spiritual issues that enable us to move away from self-centeredness. Hence, ingrown church leaders are not called first of all to be creative and clever, but rather to faith and repentance.

The medicine prescribed in this book doesn't always taste good. But in Pastor Miller's eyes it's always necessary. He shares from his understanding of Scripture as well as a lengthy and rich experience as a pastor. I, for one, am glad for his contribution.

The Action Steps and Reading Shelf at the conclusion of each chapter enhance the value of the book greatly.

Most pastors reading this book are not likely to find identifying with Pastor Miller difficult. And I suspect most will be challenged and helped.

FRANK R. TILLAPAUGH
Bear Valley Baptist Church
Denver, Colorado

ACKNOWLEDGMENTS

I am indebted for this book to more people than I could ever mention. But I especially wish to thank Bill Krispin, who suggested the title of the book; Dr. Edmund P. Clowney, who taught me the biblical concept of the church presented here; LeRoy B. Oliver, who first encouraged me to write on the subject of the ingrown church; Susan Lutz and James E. Ruark, for their editorial work; and Bill Viss and John Yenchko, for their support of this undertaking. I thank Hannah Steinberg for typing the manuscript and Jane Whitted for typing earlier drafts. With gratitude I also acknowledge the vital partnership of the members of New Life Church and other friends who have prayed for this work. Above all, anything helpful in it is due entirely to the grace of God.

"I am not ashamed of the gospel, because it is the power of God for the salvation of everyone who believes: first for the Jew, then for the Gentile."   ROMANS 1:16

"Oh, the power, the melting, conquering, transforming power of that dear cross of Christ! My brethren, we have but to abide by the preaching of it, we have but constantly to tell abroad the matchless story, and we may expect to see the most remarkable spiritual results. We need to despair of no man now that Jesus has died for sinners. With such a hammer as the doctrine of the cross, the most flinty heart will be broken; and with such a fire as the sweet love of Christ, the most mighty iceberg will be melted. We need never despair for the heathenish or superstitious races of men; if we can but find occasion to bring the doctrine of Christ crucified into contact with their natures, it will yet change them, and Christ will be their king."

CHARLES HADDON SPURGEON, THE PASSION AND DEATH OF CHRIST

"It was by Him that life began to exist, and that life was the light of mankind. So the light continues to shine in the darkness, for the darkness has never overpowered it."

JOHN 1:4–5, WILLIAMS

"You are an elect people, a royal priesthood, a holy nation, a people for God's own possession, in order that you may proclaim the praises of him who called you out of darkness into his wonderful light. Once you were not a people, but now you are the people of God; once you had not received mercy, but now you have received mercy."

1 PETER 2:9–10, WILLIAMS

"It [evangelism] . . . is to be caught within the explosion of the gospel. Christ is at work . . . and in his working we are caught, impelled, given until we become part of the lives of those to whom we are sent."

D. T. NILES, INAUGURAL SERMON, UNION THEOLOGICAL SEMINARY

I

WHERE MISSIONARY
LIFE BEGINS

CHAPTER 1

THE INGROWN CHURCH LEADER: God's Call to Faith and Repentance

This book is concerned with renewing the ingrown local church. It focuses on the way to take a church that is turned in on itself and give it an outward orientation toward the world. Much of this book is addressed to pastors, for they are crucial to any work of revival in the local church. But this study is also an urgent call for every leader in the local church to become God's change agent within his or her congregation.

The key word to describe such a leader is *pacesetter*. The word derives from the runner in a race who moves ahead of the pack and sets the example that gets others moving. Pacesetters are people who motivate an ingrown church to outreach by setting the example of a renewed leadership, people of faith who know God's will and are willing to make every sacrifice in order to fulfill it. They are the ones God uses to overcome and dismantle the barriers every congregation erects around itself to guarantee its own comfort and security.

This call to action is not based on personal interest, whim, or the possession of unique gifts for ministry, but on the definite, revealed will of the risen Lord. In declaring the Great Commission, the Savior has stood before the Church and said, "Therefore go and make disciples of all nations."[1] He is not

---

[1]Matthew 28:16–20. See also Luke 24:45–49; Acts 1:8; John 20:19–23.

proposing an elective course of action, an option for the evangelistically gifted. He is telling each of us what is our first duty. It is to disciple all nations.

Since the King has spoken, it should be clear that He expects all of us to obey His will without reservations or delay. But it should also be clear that the majority of local American congregations are, in practice, saying no to His will. They do so by ignoring it.

Still, you may ask, "Why should we have one more book on the subject of the local church and its problems with introversion and indifference?" There are many fine books today dealing with this topic.

Think, for instance, of an insightful book like *What's Gone Wrong with the Harvest?* by James F. Engel and H. Wilbert Norton, or the helpful study, *The Dynamics of Church Growth*, by Ron Jensen and Jim Stevens. And who can hope to top *The Master's Plan for Making Disciples* by Win Arn and Charles Arn, with its wealth of practical suggestions on implementing the Great Commission in the local church? And for sheer practicality, we need to go a long way to surpass the program of evangelism set forth in D. James Kennedy's *Evangelism Explosion*. If that is not enough, remember that other highly instructive studies have been contributed by such distinguished people as Donald McGavran, C. Peter Wagner, Virgil Gerber, Lyle Schaller, Edward R. Dayton, and Ted W. Engstrom. Why, then, undertake one more venture into such a well-plowed field?

STARTING THE ENGINES

Having acknowledged the value of these works, I yet insist that there are crucial failures in the *faith* of the local church and its leadership that cry out for correction. I am convinced that many congregations and their leaders are so immobilized by unbelief that concepts for ministry that would be helpful in other circumstances are relatively valueless to them.

Imagine that our situation ecclesiastically is like that of a jetliner diving to earth, with three of its four engines shut down. Collision with the ground is only ten minutes away. In this state of ultimate crisis, the pilot needs to know only one thing: how to start the engines immediately.

If he is successful and power is restored, the pilot, his crew, and the airline as a whole can profitably consider ways to improve service to their passengers. They might examine such matters as greater efficiency and friendliness in the flight attendants, faster baggage delivery, or even an improved aircraft design. But in a situation of end-time peril, the only thing worth concentrating on is the cause of the engine failure and how to correct it. Other improvements are useless if that problem is not solved first.

Ingrown churches face the same crisis of power failure and possible destruction on a spiritual level. Some of them have crashed spiritually and never noticed their own fatal ending. The evidence is easily found in lack of zeal for outreach. In some cases, congregations and their leaders have even come to suspect zeal for witness as evidence of fanaticism—or at least a sign of immaturity. Other congregations still give lip service to missions and evangelism, but inwardly they have given up—quit—having lost confidence in their being used by the Lord of the harvest to bring people to Him.

Of these doubting congregations, Kennedy Smartt, a director of Mission to North America of the Presbyterian Church in America, says, "Nothing could be sadder. Many congregations and their pastors have simply lost the hope that they could be used in their communities. They have tried an evangelistic program and it failed, and now they do not believe anything will work in their community."

Similarly, with Baptistic directness, Vance Havner has frequently noted that to be a member in good standing in today's typical evangelical church, you would need to be a backslider! In his view, faith has been withering away in our churches for a generation, and only revival can bring back the fullness of Christ and a love for the lost.

A FOUNDATION OF SOFT SAND?

Even where hope still lives in the local church, the expectation of church growth is sometimes built on the soft sand of sociological perceptions rather than faith taking hold of divine omnipotence.

I once held an evangelistic crusade in a Pennsylvania

city. The setting was typical, affluent, suburban America. During those days, an elder of the congregation was driving me down the street. He pointed toward an elevated, open space dominating the area and said, in effect, "Do you see that open area? We did a careful church growth study of our city and decided that according to church-growth principles, this location has it all—new homes nearby, easy access to main roads, and highly visible exposure to the public. It's going to make our small church into a large one."

I suspect he was right. This location, combined with the desire of the church to grow, would build the congregation into a large one. But I expressed some fears to him. I did not see clear evidence that Christ was actively present in their midst, transforming lives and opening their hearts to one another. So that week I queried the people constantly in preaching and counseling, "Is God working in your life? Are you repenting? Are you building your life on Christ's free justification and your sonship in Him—or are you loaded down with inward guilt? Have you ever done a single thing because you love Jesus? Or stopped doing anything because you love Him?"

Out of this soul-searching a number of people came to a new or a renewed faith in Christ. For the first time, some church members took an active interest in witnessing. But suppose the Holy Spirit had not intervened to bring them to repentance? What would have happened to the church-growth plans? A small ingrown church would have simply turned into a large ingrown church. I believe that would have been a travesty of church-growth principles and practices, and a grieving of the Holy Spirit.

Church growth that is not inspired by faith in Christ's power to transform lives is dangerous. Ultimately, I believe, it will prove to be as displeasing to the Head of the church as numerical stagnation. The congregation that is secularized and adds secularized members to its rolls is simply confirming itself in its indifference to the will of the Lord. To find warnings about this acute danger, perhaps we need to look to writers like Richard Lovelace more than to church-growth thinkers. Lovelace says the following:

... Pastors gradually settle down and lose interest in being change agents in the church. An unconscious conspiracy arises between their flesh and that of their congregations. It becomes tacitly understood that the laity will give pastors special honor in the exercise of their gifts, if the pastors will agree to leave their congregations' pre-Christian lifestyles undisturbed and do not call for the mobilization of lay gifts for the work of the kingdom. Pastors are permitted to become ministerial superstars. Their pride is fed and their congregations are permitted to remain herds of sheep in which each has cheerfully turned to his own way.[2]

The point is that both church members and church leaders gradually lose zeal for becoming "change agents" because of corporate evils in the local church and because of personal evils in themselves. Given the setting described by Lovelace, we find that the pastoral "superstar" is doing the tasks of the congregation and therefore does not have adequate time for his own sphere of work. Enfeebled congregations are "permitted to remain herds of sheep in which each has cheerfully turned to his own way."

So congregations and their leaders today are perilously close to losing the elementary principles of faith that motivate qualitative and quantitative church growth. I am thinking of regular and thorough meditation on the promises of God, ongoing repentance based on the intense study of Scripture, continual personal and corporate prayer, daring gospel communication and discipling, mobilizing every member's gifts for Christ's mission to the world, and each congregation working to plant daughter churches.

We grope painfully and confusedly for these basic issues of faith and action and do it without much evidence of success. The reason? We have surrendered our hearts to the familiar forms of our religious life and found comfort of soul, not in knowing God, but in knowing that our worship practices are firmly settled and nothing unpredictable will happen Sunday morning. Thus we have lost contact with the risen Christ as the source of our spiritual life, and what is worse, we

[2]*Dynamics of Spiritual Life: An Evangelical Theology of Renewal* (Downers Grove, Ill.: InterVarsity, 1979), p. 207.

are often so enfeebled that we hardly know that we are out of touch with the King. In the local church we are busy, separated from Christ's transforming presence. In our alienated busyness, we have forgotten how to live near Him and daily devote ourselves to His service with intensity. We can see this in the low burning of faith in the ingrown congregation, in the weariness written on the workers' faces, and the metronome sameness of much worship and praying.

THE CHURCH AS A RELIGIOUS CUSHION

The local church was intended by Jesus to be a gathering of people full of faith—strong in their confidence in Him—not a gathering of religious folk who desperately need reassurance. Perhaps seeking personal comfort is not wrong in itself. But it is desperately wrong when it becomes the primary reason for the existence of the local church. When that happens, the local church is no living fellowship at all, but a retreat center where anxious people draw resources that enable them merely to cope with the pains of life. The church then becomes a religious cushion.

This religious cushioning may take a number of forms. In its liberal variety, its primary concern is to comfort suburbanites with a vision of a God who is too decent to send nice people like them to hell. In its sacerdotal form, its purpose is to tranquilize the guilt-ridden person with the religious warmth of its liturgy. Among conservatives and evangelicals, its primary mission all too often is to function as a preaching station where Christians gather to hear the gospel preached to the unconverted, to be reassured that liberals are mistaken about God and hell, and to renew one's sense of well-being without having a serious encounter with the living God.

By April 1970 I had grown sick to death of the church viewed as "religious cushion" and me as chief cushioner. I had been a pastor for more than a decade and an instructor at Westminster Theological Seminary in Philadelphia for four years. I had given it all my best shot. But as a change agent I had bombed out. I was awash with cynicism about the prospects of the Christian church and went around with continual sorrow in my heart over the state of the churches around me. In a mood of dark despair I resigned both from the seminary faculty and from my pastorate at a church (hereafter called "the Chapel") in nearby Bucks County, Pennsylvania. Seeing no future for the Christian church and soured by my own failure as an instrument of change, I agreed with Pogo's comment, "We have met the enemy, and he is us."

I was in depression for several weeks. But gradually during those tearful days I came to see God, Christian people, and myself in a new light. I asked myself, "Why are you weeping?" Other questions followed. "Do you see yourself primarily as a victim?" "Are you blaming others when the basic fault may be yours?" Eventually it occurred to me that the primary failure was mine. I sensed that I had been crippled by my liking to be liked. As a result I repented of my pride, timidity, and love of peer approval. Then I understood why I had been unable to deal with the lack of zeal for Christ that I constantly encountered among my fellow Christians.

This honesty quickly began to liberate my conscience, and my witnessing became bolder. Early in May I joined a group of students from Westminster to do my first open-air preaching in Greenwich Village in New York City. I felt like a fool, but I reasoned in my heart, "So what?" So I stood on a box under the arch in Washington Square and proclaimed Christ at the top of my lungs. It was no small surprise to me to see a crowd gather and at least one person make a profession of faith in Christ.

Somehow that act of abandonment alerted me to my need to know more about the Great Commission. It seemed to me that perhaps I had been understanding it too narrowly and legalistically as a bare command of the Lord, without being gripped by His presence as the enabling power to fulfill it. Somehow I needed to grasp the Great Missionary Presence that Christ had promised in the Gospel of Matthew: "And certainly I will be with you all the days to the end of the age." In brief, I needed to learn how the promises of God, and especially Christ's promise of the Spirit, related to the missionary mandate given by the Lord before His ascension.

So, inspired by my wife Rose Marie's encouragement, she and I bought bright red sleeping bags for ourselves and three of our children. After that we headed for Spain for a summer of study. Settled in Barcelona, I began an intensive study of the promises of God in Scripture. I spent long hours tracing out great themes of grace predicted in Isaiah, Ezekiel, Jeremiah, Joel, Habakkuk, and Zechariah. Sometimes, like a man dying of thirst, I drank in the Gospel of John and the enormous promises presented in it. I was also greatly helped by reading Mrs. O. Howard Taylor's two-volume biography of Hudson Taylor and Joachim Jeremias's little book, *Jesus' Promise to the Nations*. Somehow these works helped me tie the promises of God directly to Jesus' person as the risen Lord.

I began to see that an act of faith lay at the heart of any obedience to the Great Commission. In faith we claim the presence of Christ as the power for fulfilling His missionary will. The promises are the handles that we grab in our weakness in order to secure His presence.

As the weeks passed, my mind also began to be captured by the vastness of God's promises. I was awed by what the risen Lord had promised to me in my weakness, utterly silenced in my soul like an astronomer unexpectedly seeing a whole new galaxy when he was only searching for a single planet! Our apartment, provided by generous Christian friends, overlooked the Mediterranean Sea.

After studying these great promises, I would go out on the balcony, where the sea stretched out before me. The ancients had called it "the Great Sea." I understood why, because it extended in its blue-green vastness as far as my eye could see. But this was nothing compared to what I was reading in the Scriptures. These promises were world-embracing. Christ not only said, "Go with the gospel," but also, "I will give you the power to bring in an immeasurable harvest." Often as I stood there looking at the sea, my faith was stirred by the Old Testament promise that the knowledge of the glory of the Lord will cover the *whole* earth as the waters cover the sea.[3]

Until then, I had seen the promises of Scripture more as predictive prophecy that applied either to past events like the Lord's incarnation, death, burial, and resurrection, or to future happenings associated with His second coming. I did not see

---

[3]Numbers 14:21; Isaiah 11:9; Habakkuk 2:14.

the promises as having a contemporary reference to me and the local church except in the vaguest possible way.

But while I was studying the Gospel of John, my mind was challenged by the "now-character" of promise passages like John 7:37–39. In this passage Jesus says, "If anyone thirsts, let him come to me and drink. He that believes in me, from within him, as the Scripture has said, will flow rivers of living water." John interprets this promise by applying it to the gift of the Spirit given after Jesus' glorification. He writes in verse 39, "He spoke this of the Holy Spirit, who was not yet given because Jesus was not yet glorified" (MILLER).

As I meditated on this teaching, the present significance of the promise became clear. The "rivers of living water" signified life-giving power provided from above to flow in and through the believer—power for holy living and daring witness. But there is a strong now-implication in Jesus' words. The promise of verse 38 is in the Greek present, which is not quite like our English present; it is linear, ongoing, expressing habitual or continuously present activity. In other words, Jesus was saying, "*The abundance of the Spirit is for those who are believing now and keep right on believing.*"

So "believing" is present, ongoing believing and as such is a continuing channel for receiving grace moment by moment. This was a life-changing discovery for me. Not only did it awaken my confidence in Christ's *availability* to help me, but it also began to work in me a new release from my self-dependence and self-effort.

I then *knew* with quiet, unshakable faith that these promises were mine as a servant of the King, mine to claim for life and service in His church. There was power available to change me and to turn around the ingrown church. It could be claimed by any Christian right in the present: now!

THE OUTPOURING OF THE SPIRIT

I was stimulated by reading Herman Bavinck's remarkable essay on "The Gift of the Spirit," and I traced through both Testaments the language of the outpouring of the Spirit.[4] In

[4] *Our Reasonable Faith* (Grand Rapids: Wm. B. Eerdmans, 1956), pp. 386–403.

essence the Spirit is compared to a mighty river or an overflowing stream or an artesian spring bubbling up. I had rightly discerned that this promise of Christ's fullness had a past reference to Pentecost and a future reference to the transformed world; but I had missed the emphasis in the Gospel of John on the present application of this promise to those who "are believing" or "keep believing." I had missed the fact that God wishes to use such promises to awaken us daily from our dryness to claim the Spirit's refreshing life.

When I returned from Spain to Westminster and to my congregation in early October, I determined not to act on my feelings but simply on the basis of the promises. I daily claimed them in my weakness ("thirsting") and then took my courage in my hands and talked about Christ to everyone who would listen. My teaching focused on Christ's willingness to give the Holy Spirit on an ongoing basis to us now, as we in our weakness claimed the promises in prayer.

The results were revolutionary. Before this, I had often viewed the local congregation as a jury passing judgment on my sermons and pastoral work. But after my return from Barcelona I had a new heart concern for them to enter into a life of faith, conditioned by the freedom of daily surrender to Christ and reliance on His Spirit. Within two years I saw more people converted than in the previous twenty years of my witness and ministry.

What I had discovered was God's normal expectations for the church. For the first time I saw that the normal Christian was Spirit-filled and so was the normal church, and I used that biblical vision of normality to call local churches back to God's standard for His body. I believe that it is right here that we encounter the essence of the threat to the modern congregation: its tendency to despair and defeat because it has redirected its faith toward its past or to human resources, rather than to the promises of God with their focus on the power of the Spirit to revive us. In the words of George E. Ladd, such redirecting of our faith to "human adequacy and sufficiency" puts us in the alarming position of being "an enemy of the light," a religious people who have embraced "the character of the age of this world: darkness."[5]

I have written this book to speak to the deadly peril of misdirected faith. I do so freely acknowledging my need to resist my own defeatism and my hourly need to claim the promises of God by faith. But in the midst of my own ongoing struggle, I am constrained to send a communiqué from the front. I am a church planter, and I know the battle terrain where people and pastors are living and dying, where the nature of the enemy often is obscure, where in fact we are often our own worst enemies, where disastrous mistakes are made but rarely acknowledged and forsaken, and where the deepest need is always for each member of the local church to become God's pacesetter, in zealous fulfillment of the missionary mandate given to us by our King.

I want to offer you, as a church leader, the hope that today you can become God's change agent. As your faith is stirred to action, you can become God's co-laborer in His church. You need no longer view yourself as victimized by the "system" or immobilized by the failings of others. If God can help one of His weakest sons like me, He surely can help you.

A CALL TO RADICAL COMMITMENT

So let me call you and your congregation, not simply to survival for another week, but to radical commitment: to believe Christ's promises and to do His will at all costs. That will is revealed in His command to the church to go with the gospel to the nations and make disciples of them. Our task, then, is a missionary task. This mission consists in the whole outreach enterprise of evangelizing and discipling mankind, and it involves the participation of every living member of the local congregation.

For that reason, this book looks first at the missionary purpose of the local church, next at the intellectual content of the Great Commission and its practical meaning for the local church, and then at the nature of missionary leadership in the

[5] *The Gospel of the Kingdom* (Grand Rapids: Wm. B. Eerdmans, 1959), p. 31.

congregation. From there we turn to missionary strategies in the local church and its community. Finally we will evaluate specific programs of outreach for the local church. The main divisions of the book are as follows:

I. Where Missionary Life Begins
II. Getting Our Missionary Identity Straight
III. Uncovering the Sources of Missionary Power
IV. Serving as God's Missionary Leaders
V. Discovering God's Missionary Strategies
VI. Developing God's Missionary Programs

ACTION STEPS

1. Write a brief definition of the term "pacesetter."
2. Define what is meant by "religious cushioning."
3. Evaluate yourself: To what extent are you a "pacesetter"?
4. Memorize John 7:37–39, then claim regularly in prayer Christ's promise to satisfy your thirst and enable your witness to "flow" to others.

READING SHELF

BRAUN, NEIL. "Many Members in One Body," *Laity Mobilized: Reflections on Church Growth in Japan and Other Lands.* Grand Rapids: Wm. B. Eerdmans, 1971, pp. 75–84.

ELLIOT, ELISABETH. *Shadow of the Almighty: The Life and Testament of Jim Elliot.* New York: Harper Brothers, 1958, pp. 232–49.

HYDE, DOUGLAS. *Dedication and Leadership.* Notre Dame, Ind.: University of Notre Dame Press, 1966.

LOVELACE, RICHARD F. *Dynamics of Spiritual Renewal.* Downers Grove, Ill.: InterVarsity, 1979, pp. 80–144.

MILLER, C. JOHN. *Repentance and Twentieth Century Man.* Fort Washington, Pa.: Christian Literature Crusade, 1980, pp. 9–17.

SPURGEON, CHARLES HADDON. *An All-Round Ministry.* London: Banner of Truth Trust, repr. 1972, pp. 1–31.

CHAPTER 2

THE INGROWN CHURCH: God's Call to Faith and Repentance

W. Curry Mavis writes in his book *Advancing the Smaller Church,*

> Like persons, local churches are sometimes introvertive. Following the introvertive pattern in human personality, these churches turn their interests and their energies inwardly upon themselves. They are concerned primarily with their own affairs. Sometimes they devote most of their attention to spiritual introspection which results in a neglect of spiritual expression in their communities.[1]

Mavis seems right on target with his analysis of the inward-looking congregation. Stimulated by his insights, I did a paper for my denomination's home missions board in 1965, entitled "How to Overcome Introversion in the Small Church." I attempted to show that many of the characteristics of the small church resemble those of a small tribal group. Though I was encouraged by an enthusiastic response to the paper from pastors and other church leaders, I knew even then that it lacked something foundational.

By the time I had returned to the Chapel in the fall of 1970, I understood what my diagnosis lacked. From my own experiences as a pastor and church member, I had a rather firm

---

[1] W. Curry Mavis, *Advancing the Smaller Church* (Grand Rapids: Baker, 1957), p. 30.

grasp on the essential features of the ingrown church; I discerned that these qualities were in some degree deviations from the norm of the New Testament church. But before this I had not clearly seen that the introverted church reflected members' unbelieving resistance to the will of the King, as expressed by His missionary mandate. After Spain I saw the introverted church no longer as partly out of line with the divine will, but radically disobedient to it. At the same time I realized that the ingrown church was missing out in respect to the Lord's missionary presence, which enables congregations to fulfill the Great Commission.

In my preaching and teaching I began to stress that the missionary command has two sides: (1) a command to go and disciple (an impossible task), and (2) a promise from Jesus to be with us as we obey the command (the power to do: an impossible task). I underscored the Father's willingness to give the Holy Spirit to believers as they prayed.[2] I also focused attention on the normal church member as a person who believes. This believer is filled with the Spirit for bold witness, and the normal church is a place where many believers comprise a power center of praise, prayer, and effective outreach with the gospel (1 Thess. 1–2).

But the crucial thing I brought to the members of our church and to my seminary students was *a willingness to talk with them personally.* About what? About the nature and power of Christ's ministry through His missionary Spirit— always raising searching questions of a personal sort.[3] I really did what *any* pacesetting church member can do. For example, I asked church officers questions like, "What do you think about our church? Do you see us like the church described in Acts or Thessalonica? What do you see as the essential features of our church? Do we have a problem with unbelief? What is the specific purpose that God has for us as a local church?"

I also approached church members and asked them, "Are you growing spiritually? Do you see yourself bearing the fruit of the Spirit? Have you repented of any sins lately?"

As a result of these conversations, we as a congregation

---

[2] Luke 11:1–13; Acts 1:13–14; 2:1; 4:23–31; Philippians 1:19.
[3] See also John 4:10, 13.

were compelled to face the issue of our ingrownness and to raise searching questions about its roots, not just in our religious sociology, but in our corporate and individual unbelief. We seemed to be, on the one hand, indifferent to the Great Commission as a command; on the other, ignorant of it as a Great Promise, insensitive to the Father's willingness to give us the Holy Spirit in response to our earnest prayer. Through this diagnostic interaction, seven core elements of introversion began to emerge, qualities we paid scant attention to. We had accepted them as normal marks of any small congregation, not as dangerous symptoms of a deeply rooted unbelief. These qualities are as follows:

1. Tunnel Vision

Members of the ingrown church body are characterized by tunnel vision that limits potential ministries of the church to those that can be accomplished by the visible, human resources at hand. These possibilities are often further limited by recollections of past negative experiences and perceptions of present obstacles. At bottom, this is unbelief based on a secularized ignorance of the Spirit's power—His ability to supply us with God's goals for the church and the supernatural means to reach them.

This unbelief expresses itself in the quiet acceptance of churchly dullness as normal, and numerical stagnation or decline as inevitable. The amazing picture of the "greater works" Christian drawn by Jesus in the Gospel of John is never seriously considered as a possibility for the life of the church and its members (John 14:12–14 MILLER). Jesus' startling promise that His disciples would do greater works than He did in His public ministry is simply not a part of the religious vision of the ingrown church member.

Today such a foreshortened vision reveals itself most conspicuously in our indifference to the *peril* of the lost. People are no longer seen as being in danger of perishing forever under the condemnation of a holy God. Win Arn and Charles Arn, in their book *The Master's Plan for Making Disciples,* say bluntly, "The biblical concept of 'lostness' has disappeared from the conscience of most churches and most

Christians." They conclude, "Little remains of the first-century Christian's burning conviction that without Christ, every person is forever lost."[4]

2. Shared Sense of Group Superiority

W. Curry Mavis notes in his book that this visionless church is often characterized by a sense of superiority to "the others." He observes that many smaller congregations and their leadership have become egocentric because of "their fear of extinction." In his view, "struggling churches are likely to exaggerate points of superiority they actually possess as means of compensation for their limitations."[5] What they do is build an attitude of superiority over others by elevating a positive feature in the church life or tradition and then comparing this feature with groups which lack this quality.

Sometimes the self-exaltation concentrates on the unique history of the congregation or denomination, or on the heroic sufferings of founding fathers. In other instances, pride arises out of superior knowledge of the Scriptures and "deeper spirituality" of the members of the congregation. Some fundamentalists strongly emphasize their godly separation from the world, with separation defined by not doing things—drinking, smoking, dancing, and attending movie theaters—and consequently feeling superior to "worldly sinners." Astonishingly, I have known more than one congregation that had heavily invested the pride of the church in its cemetery. The graveyard was the center of its glory, proving that the church belonged to an ancient and superior tradition of the best Christian people.

Thus the assumed positive feature leads to an unconscious elitist attitude. The result is that Christ is offended and withdraws His power and presence from the meetings, for this grace is for the humble, not for the self-exalting and self-satisfied. If we are proudly clinging to an ecclesiastical tradition and making it our hope, we may have secured our status in our own eyes yet failed miserably with the Lord.

---

[4] *The Master's Plan for Making Disciples* (Pasadena: Church Growth Press, 1982), p. 8.
[5] *Advancing the Smaller Church*, p. 32.

3. Extreme Sensitivity to Negative Human Opinion

I have said that the inward-looking church is frequently characterized by a sense of spiritual superiority. Paradoxically, the members of the ingrown church are also likely to feel inferior and shrivel up and die at the first sign of opposition. A word of disapproval from a "pillar" of the church is enough to rattle the ecclesiastical squirrel cage and send everyone running for cover.

Behind this timidity is the suspicion that intense spiritual conflict is inherently unspiritual. Sometimes there is good reason for this fear. Church conflicts can be merely personality clashes. As such they can be horrid affairs, and before I came to the Chapel there had been a number of such worldly wars in the church. But as John R. W. Stott has pointed out in his book *Christ the Controversialist,* Jesus in His ministry certainly did not avoid conflict on what He considered to be major issues concerning the kingdom of God.

The sad truth is that one negative critic with a loud voice who speaks from within the inner circle of the ingrown church usurps the role of Christ, wielding the power to make or break programs. It may be an aggressive young man reacting to some of his own lawless excesses and now trying to impose a yoke of legalism on the whole congregation. It may be a conservative elder who has no confidence in the Holy Spirit's power to supply finances and consistently votes against any attempt to renovate the church building or relocate in a more promising area. I have seen a youth program stifled by an older woman who felt threatened by the unwashed types showing up at the meetings.

Whatever form the opposition takes, we will discover that an ingrown church has given in for so long to intimidation that its fears have obscured vital contact with the promises of God. As a result, fear casts out love for "a world that is falling apart," a world that desperately needs a community of love.[6]

The problem is that the people of God and their leaders have often gone a long time without seeing the Face of faces,

---

[6]David Watson, *I Believe in Evangelism* (Grand Rapids: Wm. B. Eerdmans, 1976), p. 138.

and therefore any angry human face, or even a disapproving word, wipes them out. Often, behind this religious cowardice lies a refusal to accept suffering and unpopularity as a cost of pacesetting church growth. Regrettably, this excessive fear of conflict also means that ineffective church programs keep rolling on like Old Man River. In *What's Gone Wrong with the Harvest?* Engel and Norton express their conviction that this compulsive orientation to traditional programs, and the accompanying fear of resistance to change, results in "smoothly running harvest equipment, except that there are no cutting blades."[7]

4. Niceness in Tone

Allied to the exaggerated fear of controversy in the ingrown church is the shared desire to be seen as "nice." Upon coming to the Chapel, I soon gained the reputation in the church and community as a "nice pastor." That meant I was now an insider and not a threat to anyone. In itself there is nothing wrong with being accepted because you are viewed as gentle and kindly. Indeed, each Christian should diligently seek to be all of that. But what is often wanted in the local church is unrelieved blandness: a "nice pastor" preaching "nice sermons" about a "nice Jesus" delivered in a "nice tone" of voice.

What is twisted about all this is that "niceness" is being substituted for Christ's holy love, a heroic quality that might not in some circumstances prove to be nice at all. What we really want is to be comfortable and undisturbed. "Nice" is just another way of being *safe*.

In C. S. Lewis's *The Lion, the Witch, and the Wardrobe*, Susan asks about Aslan, the great lion who is a Christ-figure in the book. She inquires, "Is he—quite safe?" The answer must be, "'Course he isn't safe. But he's good. He's the King, I tell you."

So it is with Christ the King. He isn't safe! Hence it is likely that those who are walking with Him in close fellowship

---

[7] James P. Engel and H. Wilbert Norton, *What's Gone Wrong with the Harvest? A Communication Strategy for the Church and World Evangelism* (Grand Rapids: Zondervan, 1975), p. 30.

will not always be nice and predictable. But the introverted church wants to secure the church doors against divine surprises and unannounced entrances by the King.

In one such instance, a pastor in a mainline church decided to do a daring thing by preaching on John 3:3 and the "new birth." During his sermon a woman parishioner came under deep conviction from God and found herself irresistibly drawn forward. She said later, "I was so moved by the desire to know God that I simply could not sit in the pew. But when the pastor saw me walking down the aisle toward him, he asked, 'What is it?' I answered, 'I need Christ so very much. Please tell me how to get this new birth.' "

The shocked minister, after a moment's pause, chose to ignore her and went on with his sermon. The woman fell on her knees before the communion table and stayed there through the rest of the sermon, the collection of the offering, and the benediction. Afterward the congregation filed out without a single person, not even the pastor, coming to talk to her. What we had there was a churchly conspiracy to make God and Christ something other than what they are. Christ is not a nice, tame God who can be controlled, caged lest He intrude in unseemly ways on Sunday mornings or in other church affairs.

5. Christian Soap Opera in Style

The niceness of the inward-looking church does not go deep enough to hinder the soap-opera style in which many a congregational life is lived. Soap operas are basically a series of endlessly repeated conversations, and gossip (for that is what it is) is often the only kind of "body life" an ingrown church knows.

In the introverted church we find that the members use their tongues a great deal—not to witness or pray or praise or to affirm one another, but to publicly review one another's flaws, doings, and sins. We all know how easy it is for church members to go home after hearing a sermon and have "roast pastor" for lunch.

But why is this so? Part of the answer is that gossip is a cruel lust and has in it all the perverted satisfaction that a lust can provide. But the deeper answer is that unbelief and fear characterize the mental outlook in the ingrown church. The members of the church do not see themselves as living, praying, and talking in partnership with Christ and one another through His indwelling Holy Spirit. There is often a failure to cultivate among leaders and people a spirit of forgiveness, mutual forbearance, and love. In brief, there is a shortage of real love in the congregation, a love fueled by a faith that has rejected the temptation to gossip.

The result is that as long as the gossip is "nice" in tone, church people believe they can go around saying the most dreadful things about other Christians. I am not thinking about wishy-washy churches where adultery or drunkenness are tolerated, but strict churches where you would get your walking papers for committing gross sins like that. Yet in such congregations gossip has become so normal that to stand against it would be interpreted as arrogance and a rejection of fellowship.

In a congregation I served before the Chapel, I once overheard a visitor to one of our services tell this story to a young father. He said, "This morning you have brought your child to be given over to the Lord. I did that once too. But let me urge you from the bottom of my heart, don't do to your child what I did to mine. As he grew up, he listened to me criticize the pastor year after year. As a consequence, I turned off my boy to the church and to ministers, and today he is far from God."

With something like a physical spasm he added, "I plead with you: don't ever criticize your pastor and other Christians, or you will destroy your son too."

If you criticize others in the church, you are really attacking yourself—because we are one body in Christ. Indeed, to attack others with our tongue is really to attack Him, the Head of the church. So when gossip rages, what is lost is not only reputation, but the whole life of faith that expresses itself through love in the local church community.

6. Confused Leadership Roles

In many churches the members of the congregation do not want officers who are trying to be pacesetters for God's kingdom. This is especially true of the small church, where fear of change often runs high. The reason for this should be clear. In the typical self-centered church there is a hidden determination to eradicate enthusiasm that disturbs the comfortable routine dictated by self-trust, self-exaltation, niceness as a defense mechanism, and the rights of gossip. Zeal for Christ's global missionary cause in a leader is hard for old wineskins to handle. Such fermenting (when it is not inspired by unsound doctrine or evil motives) is hard to warehouse without its breaking forth and upsetting the status quo.

Therefore the pastor and his wife are expected to act within the bounds of an unexpressed but nonetheless clearly defined social contract. This contract is between the pastor and the congregation and to some degree between him and the local community. It states that the congregation will support, honor, and pay the pastor and his wife as long as they are inspiring yet dignified, sweet but saltless. In return, the pastor, assisted by his spouse, is expected to do all the real work of the local church—that is, he is expected to do his own work and everyone else's too. The net effect is that he moves at an exhausting pace that leaves no time for witnessing, solid study of the Scriptures, prayer, and the meditation that builds faith filled with the fire of God's presence.

In this system elders also lack great convictions about God and His gospel and have little active role in the daily lives of church members. Deacons major in mechanical matters like taking up the offering, caring for the building, and sending infrequent gifts of money to the distant poor of Ethiopia. There is no room for the biblical zeal of the ancient prophets or the apostles. What the church actually wants is a pastor and elders who have the majesty and manner of Moses and Aaron but none of the prophetic fire. The sad result is that the fundamental idea that every Christian is a priest and minister serving God is almost entirely submerged. Where nothing is expected of church members in this regard, little is given.

7. A Misdirected Purpose

It is clear from the foregoing that the controlling purpose in the ingrown church has to do with *survival*—not with growth through the conversion of the lost. The ingrown church has a distorted unity of concern, a dominating priority, in spite of its divisions and factions. The unity is essentially that of the comfortable, private club determined to protect its institutional values and privileges. In the churchly club the members are attempting to defend traditional group values in the face of "outsiders" who are perceived as likely to subvert their traditions or to be the kind of people "you would not want your daughter to marry." At the center of this tribal exclusiveness is the fixed order of Sunday worship, sociability, and devotion to the church building as the sacred clubhouse.

We can recognize this misdirected purpose by noting what goes into the church budget (and what is left out) and how visitors to the church services are welcomed. Visitors to the inward-looking congregation may be given a formal welcome and a smile, but the heart is not in it. Neither is the head. No planning is devoted to finding ways to assimilate visitors into the fellowship.

Where this distortion of purpose prevails, the danger is that eventually the church will make its own life, programs, and traditions into its object of worship. The church will give to itself the honor that belongs to God alone. What began as a way of surviving becomes blasphemous worship, with the revered aspects of the church having the claims on hearts that should be reserved exclusively for the living God.

THE PLACE TO BEGIN

Many of these seven qualities became clear to me while I was pastor at the Chapel. I do not mean to suggest that I was personally guilty of all these failings or that the church was either. But as we talked together about these issues, we faced up to an inescapable fact: we cannot change unless we know where we are and where we should be. Honesty about our aversion to God's purpose is the most important ingredient in repentance.

How do you begin to discuss these issues in your church? I suggest that you use some of the materials in this chapter for congregation appraisal. You will also profit in reading about the model of the church described in John R. W. Stott's book

Our Guilty Silence. It can be humbling to compare one's church with this active Anglican congregation in the center of London. I also recommend Robert A. Coleman's *The Master Plan of Evangelism* and the chapter entitled "Purpose" in *Dynamics of Church Growth,* by Ron Jensen and Jim Stevens.

My own experience at the Chapel in the fall of 1970 should encourage you to undertake a period of discussion. During October I prayed and talked quietly with people about the issue of our shared introversion. Nothing much seemed to happen, except that one woman whom I'll call Roberta started avoiding me. Then in early November I received a phone call. The caller said, "Roberta Peace is in the hospital having convulsions nonstop."

In answer to prayer, the convulsions stopped, and at the hospital bedside Roberta told me with an uneasy smile, "I've been avoiding you."

I laughed with her, and together we had a wonderfully open conversation in which she confessed frankly that she was terribly afraid of a close relationship with God. But she also said, "You know, I just might die from these convulsions."

As we prayed together day after day, I began to read Romans 1 to Roberta. I read it to her for ten days in a row! I fully and repeatedly explained free justification by faith and challenged her to make sure she was in Christ by faith and free from fears of judgment by God. "You cannot have it both ways," I said, "You are either in Christ by faith or in the world by unbelief."

At the end of ten days she said that her whole life was changed by a simple surrender of her life in faith to Christ and His "alien righteousness."

The change in Roberta was so dramatic, her joy so full in spite of the pain, that other church members and seminary students began to be troubled and then infected by her radiant faith. She became Christ's pacesetter while lying in a hospital bed. Conversions began to take place within and without the Chapel. By the end of six months a prominent lay leader in the church took a partner into his business so that he could devote himself to helping me in the ministry of evangelism and discipleship. As faith grew, introversion withered away.

It was all very low-key at the beginning, just a time of

diagnosis with a focus on the gospel and the promises of God. It was a good way to begin, and it was only a beginning.

ACTION STEPS

1. Using the seven core elements of introversion, evaluate yourself, your church leaders, and your congregation.

   F = Failure (Total)   **O = Outstanding**

	You	Leaders	Congregation
Darkened vision	F 1 2 3 4 5 0	F 1 2 3 4 5 0	F 1 2 3 4 5 0
Group superiority	F 1 2 3 4 5 0	F 1 2 3 4 5 0	F 1 2 3 4 5 0
Fear of negative opinions	F 1 2 3 4 5 0	F 1 2 3 4 5 0	F 1 2 3 4 5 0

2. Repent of specific sins in your life revealed by your answers in the previous evaluation.
3. Discuss the seven core elements with a fellow church member or church leader and together evaluate yourselves and your church.
4. Read "Purpose" (ch. III) in *Dynamics of Church Growth* and write a proposed purpose statement for your church.

READING SHELF

ARN, WIN, and CHARLES ARN. *The Master's Plan for Disciple Making.* Pasadena: Church Growth Press, 1982.

CHARLES E. FULLER INSTITUTE OF CHURCH GROWTH, Box 989, Pasadena, CA 91102. (Write for materials on developing purpose statements.)

GETZ, GENE A. *The Measure of a Church.* Glendale, Calif.: Regal Books, 1973.

JENSEN, RONALD. *How to Succeed the Biblical Way.* Wheaton, Ill.: Tyndale House, 1981, pp. 109–116.

SCHALLER, LYLE. *Parish Planning.* Nashville: Abingdon, 1971.

STOTT, JOHN R. W. *Our Guilty Silence.* Downers Grove: InterVarsity, 1969, pp. 57–88.

II

GETTING
OUR MISSIONARY
IDENTITY STRAIGHT

CHAPTER 3

THE LOCAL CHURCH:
Its Missionary Character

"Jack, you can't mean what you just said—that the gospel can change anyone! It can help ordinary people like you and me, but only the medical experts can help people who are psychologically damaged—like the people who want to commit suicide."

"Why do you say that, Harold?" I asked.

"Because there was a woman in our church who took her life. No one but trained professionals—medical experts—could have helped her."

I was concluding the last of three Sunday evening lectures as guest speaker in a church in May 1971. Harold, the pastor of the church, suddenly came to his feet to argue that I was mistaken to believe that the gospel could turn around people who were mentally disturbed, suicidal, addicted to drugs or alcohol, or inclined to be criminal. His action surprised everyone, but it sparked mini-debates across the church auditorium. I could hear some vigorous arguments going on as people took Harold's side or mine.

Later that evening I was sitting at home drinking tea with Rose Marie and a student from Westminster. I was left in a thoughtful mood by Harold's obvious unbelief. He just did not believe that people with serious and destructive kinks could be helped by the message of the Cross. As I drank my tea, I asked myself, "Do you *really* believe that Christ's gospel can change anyone who believes it—or was that just talk on your part?"

By this time I had seen that the key weakness in the introverted church is the unbelieving timidity of its members. But was my own confidence really all that great in the power of the Cross to change anyone who would receive it? Was I willing to take the "risks" that such confidence required? Would I, for instance, welcome people who were suicidal to our church? Into our lives and home?

I needed to pray. I don't think the others in the room had any idea of the collision of values going on within me. I had seen how God had radically transformed the life of a Roberta Peace, but how far could one carry this transformation business? I asked the others to pray with me, and I quietly surrendered any further reservations in my heart to God and asked Him to remove my fears. I then committed myself to acting on the principle that the gospel can change anyone who will take it to heart. As I prayed, I had a mysterious yearning to see Christ glorified through the changes He would work in damaged persons who would embrace Him through the gospel.

What was happening in me is that I was beginning to shed my own "ingrownness." I wanted to become a more effective pacesetter in my local church. I was slowly learning that to do it, you must look upward to God and rely exclusively on His power. I needed to humble myself and get my own identity straight. I needed to see that I belonged to God first of all and so did the church, and since I had this unique relationship with Him as His child, I should be willing to undergo any suffering necessary for glory to be brought to His name. I yearned that this zeal for God's glory might become, not a fitful impulse, but a permanent passion in my life.

Through the teaching of Dr. Edmund P. Clowney, then president of Westminster Seminary, I had intellectually understood that the nature of the church is defined by its being the unique possession of God, His people indwelt by Him. I understood too that His purpose for His people was that they might make His glory known, through the gospel, to all nations. But now this God-centered nature of the church and its missionary purpose took on fresh intellectual clarity and also became a living fire within me. What I knew and felt at that time is stated succinctly in 1 Peter 2:9–10. It reads,

> But you are a chosen people, a royal priesthood, a holy nation, *a people for God's own possession* [nature of the church], in order that *you may declare the praises of him who called you* out of darkness into His marvelous light [missionary purpose]. Once you were not a people, but now you are the people of God; once you had not obtained mercy, but now you have obtained mercy (MILLER).

THE BASIC NATURE OF THE CHURCH

What, then, is the basic, fundamental nature of the church? To serve itself and its own self-centered interests? Or even first of all to serve others? No, its fundamental character is to belong to God. In this passage Peter says that we are "a people for God's own possession" (Hebrew *am*, Greek *laos*).

The language "people of God" presupposes an Old Testament background of the exodus from Egypt led by divine power and a call to be the covenant people of God at Mount Sinai.[1] The living, transcendent God came to claim Israel as His special possession, an act that prefigured the Spirit's coming at Pentecost to make the church the new people of God. Peter squelches the idea that the church has a right to exist for its own egocentric interests and comforts. It exists for God, and He in His infinite majesty lives in it as a troubling, transforming, barrier-breaking presence.

But there is more implied in this passage. Who are the subjects of this splendid action of redemption? Not Jews sanctified by centuries of law-keeping, but the raw, unwashed Gentiles.[2] The idea is that God has taken them to His own great, loving heart and has written over them "Mine." They are immeasurably and inexpressibly exalted. *They are God-possessed.*

Those who are the God-possessed by virtue of their new life and relationship to God are also holy. Peter says that the "people for God's own possession" are "a holy nation." That

---

[1] Exodus 6:6–8; 19:1–6; 20–24.
[2] 1 Peter 2:10; 4:3.

is, if we belong to a holy God we are inherently involved in His holiness by virtue of that relationship. Because God lives in these transformed sinners, they are sanctified by His presence and distinguished from the world.

In his perceptive book, *The Missionary Nature of the Church*, Johannes Blauw says that the expression "a holy nation" as applied to the church "suggests that the Gentiles, unholy in themselves, have been sanctified in coming to Christ." He adds, "By this means they have separated themselves from the others, the disobedient, and now stand in a positive relationship to God."[3] Thus the God-possessed are *the God-separated*, consecrated to Him and distinguished from the world.

"A ROYAL PRIESTHOOD"

I have shown in the first two chapters that the introverted church is characterized by much religious presumption, but that its fragile religiosity masks despair and deeply felt guilt. Returning to 1 Peter 2:9, we see that this problem is also dealt with by divine action. The God-possessed and God-separated are the *God-accepted*. They are called "a royal priesthood," terminology that signals their premier closeness to God as His own dear people. What has brought these who are far off near to the divine presence? It is not their good works or religious activity. This new people of God, this new Israel, has been reconciled to Him through faith in "the precious blood of Christ" (1 Peter 1:19).

In the former covenant made with Moses and the people of Israel, the command was always, "Do not come any closer" (Ex. 3:5). But now, through faith in the Cross these defiled and corrupted people are brought near to God. They do not make this passage from death to life by way of a great deal of religious grunting and groaning, but by an act of faith in Christ and His work. This is not because their faith is so powerful, but because the blood sacrifice of Christ is such a powerful atonement for sins. It is precious blood to Peter and to the new

---

[3] *The Missionary Nature of the Church: A Survey of the Biblical Theology of Mission* (New York: McGraw-Hill, 1962), p. 131.

people of God, but it is also precious blood to the Father, because it represents the blood of the covenant that now sanctifies this new people of God (1 Peter 6:12). As such it guarantees that His wrath is forever turned aside from those who believe in His Son.

This friendship with the holy Father is called "a royal priesthood," and it means that everyone who has trusted in Christ has ongoing access to God. There is no longer a segregated priesthood representing the people of God in worship and service; now every believer is a priest. Each believer has authority ("royal") and first-class worship rights ("priesthood"). There are no back rows with God for any believer. We are all His ministers as part of the one people of God, a truth that cuts right across the passivity in worship, prayer, and service so characteristic of the turned-in church.[4]

To summarize, the nature of the church is not first of all to serve itself, but God. Every one of us has a part in this service, because we all belong to Him, are sanctified by Him, and are accepted by Him. This is our identity as Christians belonging to the local church. We are the holy people of God, offering sacrifices of prayer and praise and good deeds through the merits of Christ. As we do this, we must not lose our God-centered identity by reducing the church and its gospel to the world's level as happened so blatantly at the World Council of Churches meeting in Uppsala, Sweden, in 1968. There the study guide for the missions study section presupposed that the church is really the servant of the world rather than of God, and has no final, unchangeable message to give to the lost. But the nature of the church is not first of all a servant of the world in the sense advocated by a Colin Williams [5] or a community of revolutionary action as held by Gustavo Gutierrez.[6] It is God's possession, and it is that *immutable* identification that qualifies its life, service, and warfare in the world.

But how exactly do we define the purpose of the church?

[4] See John R. W. Stott, *One People* (London: Falcon Books, 1969), and Hendrik Kraemer, *The Theology of the Laity* (London: Lutterworth, 1958).

[5] Colin Williams, *Where in the World? Changing Forms of the Church's Witness* (New York: National Council of Churches, 1963).

[6] Gustavo Gutierrez, *A Theology of Liberation: History, Politics* (Maryknoll, N.Y.: Orbis, 1973).

Earlier I said that the goal of the church is to glorify God in the world. First Peter accentuates this view. The church is God's own people with what Blauw has called a "directedness" in relationship to a "service of witness to mankind."[7] The church in the world is therefore "a people for God's own possession *in order that* you may declare the praises of him who called you out of darkness into his marvelous light." Peter could have used a weaker conjunction here to indicate mere result, i.e., "so that." But he did not do so. The subordinate conjunction he used is much stronger and can be translated "in order that you may thus" declare the praises of Him. . . .[8]

Blauw notes that the purpose of this revelation of the divine glory is to confront the world's darkness with the gospel. I would add that this is a head-on confrontation between the world and the deeds ("the praises") of God. They are produced by the Holy Spirit's application of the gospel to the lives of sinners. The divine glory is the difference between the former deeds of these who were once deeply stained sinners "living in debauchery, lust, drunkenness, orgies, carousing, and detestable idolatry" and their deeds now that they have become the holy people of God. This glory shines into the world's darkness as a confronting power, and more of the world's unwashed are saved as their consciences are stirred by seeing the renewed lives of God's people.

Let's apply this line of thought to the typical static congregation. This church is segregated from the world in all the wrong ways—its members exclude others by the social discipline of a private club. But though the world has often been excluded in this regrettable manner, its mindset has had full sway in a secularized local church. Church members have no eye of faith to see and act upon the promises of God. The people of such a congregation probably agree unconsciously with my pastor friend Harold and have no confidence that the gospel can rescue from spiritual, moral, and emotional destruction those who receive it by faith. They are not about to confront the world with the glory of the divine working in their lives individually or corporately. The cost is far too high for their enfeebled faith.

[7] Blauw, *The Missionary Nature of the Church*, p. 128.
[8] Ibid.

But if these church members are born-again believers, they have the Spirit, and if they have the Spirit of grace, they can be activated to declare the divine glory in the face of the world's darkness. It follows that if they cannot be stimulated by sound teaching to confront the world's darkness, it is at least possible that they themselves are still living in that darkness.

Approaching people from that standpoint, Rose Marie and I decided in 1971 to take into our home two young women, both judged to be "hopeless cases" by medical authorities. With Harold's words still ringing in our ears, we welcomed into our home Tina, twenty-two years old, a slender blond who seemed "nice." Shortly afterward, Mary came to live with us also, a sixteen-year-old brunette with an impish grin and a temper alleged to be sufficient to put Mount St. Helens to shame. On July 3, 1971, she came to us straight from a Pennsylvania state hospital, where she was said to have beaten a woman psychiatrist.

We quickly discovered that by nature they both were much like ourselves—intensely self-centered and given to various techniques of manipulation. We shared with them how Christ had helped us with similar problems, and we confronted their "spoiled child" approach to life by assigning them tasks to do in our home. We combined that with a direct challenge to both of them to receive the gospel as Christ's power to change them.

Borrowing language from Clair Davis, at that time my colleague at Westminster, I told the eruptive sixteen-year-old that she was "not a lemon but a sinner" and as a sinner she could be helped by the gospel. The gospel was designed to help those who are alienated from God by rebellious attitudes and actions. Tina, the blond girl, told us that she had made about fifty decisions for Christ at various retreats and youth camps while growing up. She said, in essence, "I am a Christian but Christ does not seem to help me very much."

Our challenge to Tina became increasingly direct. I asked her gently but persistently, "Tina, do you really know what it involves to receive Christ? Do you see any of the fruit of the Spirit in your life? Have you ever done anything because you love Him?" She became very thoughtful as she pondered these issues.

A few days later, after a time of intense prayer by Rose Marie and me for her conversion, Tina trusted her life to Christ and renounced her self-centeredness. She immediately pitched in as an ally to help us work with Mary and began to do housework with a new attitude of freedom. Her highly visible change had an indirect influence on the other girl. In many ways Tina's life began to resemble that of Roberta, and it touched the volatile Mary and made her much easier to handle. Shortly thereafter she too appeared to undergo a major change in her attitudes and behavior.

I invited Tina to give her testimony to a Monday night Bible study that had been attracting increasing numbers of non-Christians. What she had to say was remarkably God-glorifying, and evocative of praise from all who heard it. She related simply and clearly how she had seen herself as a Christian because of her repeated "decisions for Christ" but had no idea of the inward evil ruling her life. She added that she had not understood that faith had at its heart a simple trust and resting in Christ. "It woke me up to my rebelling and dislike of God," she concluded, "when Jack kept asking me all those searching questions." As a result of Tina's pacesetting testimony, a number of visitors to the Bible study became serious inquirers about the way of salvation, and two or three were brought to Christ.

TWO CHANGES AT THE CHAPEL

There was an effect on the Chapel's worship services too. The church had a traditional pattern of Sunday morning worship with a fixed order of liturgy, and I was careful not to drop any of this or move any of the elements of worship. But with the agreement of the elders, I introduced two changes.

First, people who were recently converted or had undergone marked growth were regularly given opportunity to glorify Christ by explaining how His gospel and His Spirit had changed them. The sense of God's glory as the main reason for our worshiping together increased dramatically as a result of these testimonies. Both the damaged types, like drug addicts and the suicidal, and the more-together people told how Christ had convicted them of sin and forgiven them and healed their lives.

The second new element was a sharing of the pastoral prayer with a number of men. These were men I had been teaching about prayer. They would gather to pray with me before the service. Then during the worship service they would participate in the pastoral prayer. This new outpouring of praise and prayer contributed much to the awakening of all of us to the greatness of God and our rights of access as a "royal priesthood." We were becoming a worshiping community of joy.

These main issues were coming through to people in our church and our community:

1. Our identity is that of God's own people, and our purpose in the world is to glorify Him by declaring the gospel to others.

2. You are either in Christ or not—there is no middle, neutral ground.

3. If you are in Christ, you are alive, and this new life should be bringing glory to God by your deeds of love.

4. If you are not in Christ, *now* is the time to receive Him, because you will perish if you die without knowing Him.

5. The gospel is good news—indeed, supremely good news—which believed and acted upon produces a whole new life of praise for *anyone*, no matter how corrupted, confused, or damaged.

At this point you may be tempted to shrug off all this evangelical enthusiasm as something better confined to my own theological tradition. But perhaps we all use our theological traditions to remain indifferent to biblical teaching and to protect ourselves from God's work in our midst. In response to such an objection I call attention to the experience of the Anglican Church in India during the first half of this century. Vednayakam Samuel Azariah became bishop of Dornakal, the smallest diocese in the subcontinent. By the time he died at the end of World War II, the diocese had become the largest in all India.

What made the difference? Many things. Azariah stressed

the importance of Bible knowledge being systematically im-parted in all the churches. He focused on leadership training, regular evangelism crusades after the harvests, and the use of native Indian cultural forms of worship and music. But he did something else that was supremely important. He insisted that every congregation and every church member get their identity straight. He stressed continually that each congregation was Christ's and distinct from the world. He struck the familiar note we find in 1 Peter that we are God's church in the world for a missionary purpose. Often Azariah would dramatize the need for outgoing witness when he arrived in a congregation by asking every Christian in the church building to stand up and put his or her hands on their heads and say, "I am a baptized Christian. Woe is me if I preach not the gospel![9] No wonder church members took seriously their calling to witness for God's glory! The issue is not my theological look versus yours, but a question of God's will.

Today Tina lives in New York and is happily married to a pastor. Harold is selling real estate, having left the pastorate not long after our encounter in May 1971. One of the young people in the meeting when Harold challenged me is now a missionary in Uganda. The brunette has had her ups and downs, but is able to carry on in life by herself. Much more could be said, but the point is that all of this came about at a certain cost. What it requires is a willingness as a church member to practice the art of gentle confrontation of people with the message of the gospel and the evidence of its transforming power. Of course, it will bring persecution.

A young man came to Christ as a result of Tina's testimony in early July 1971. His mother turned on me with a bitter spirit and continued for a number of years to be my enemy. She really hated me for persuading her son to become a religious enthusiast. But it was all worth it, for today there is a letter in my files written by this angry mother. In it she thanks me for enduring her hatred and persecution. She said that she was made so restless by Christ and the questions I once asked her that she finally gave in and trusted her life to Christ. She

[9]Cited in Neil S. Braun, *Laity Mobilized: Reflections on Church Growth in Japan and Other Lands* (Grand Rapids: Wm. B. Eerdmans, 1971).

writes, "I cannot describe the joy it has brought to me." I can't either. It is our joy and Christ's glory all the way.

ACTION STEPS

1. Define the nature or identity of the church, including in your definition the three qualities mentioned in 1 Peter 2:9–10.
2. Do the same for the purpose of the church.
3. What were the "main issues" coming through in the Chapel? Name one way that the discovery that there is "no neutral ground" could help revive your church.
4. Bishop Azariah dramatized every member's duty to witness. Think of a way your church could dramatize this idea in a way appropriate to your congregation.

READING SHELF

BLAUW, JOHANNES. *The Missionary Nature of the Church: A Survey of the Biblical Theology of Mission.* New York: McGraw-Hill, 1962.

BRAUN, NEIL. *Laity Mobilized: Reflections on Church Growth in Japan and Other Lands.* Grand Rapids: Wm. B. Eerdmans, 1971.

CLOWNEY, EDMUND P. *The Biblical Doctrine of the Church.* Philadelphia: Westminster Theological Seminary, 1976. Class syllabus.

GETZ, GENE A. *Sharpening the Focus of the Church.* Chicago: Moody, 1976.

STOTT, JOHN R. W. *One People.* London: Falcon Books, 1969.

CHAPTER 4

THE LOCAL CHURCH:
Its Missionary Authority

In my own theological tradition, the marks of the church are said to be the preaching of sound doctrine, pure administration of the sacraments, and the practice of church discipline.[1] Reflecting critically on this limited view of the church, Richard R. De Ridder says, "From this viewpoint the Church becomes only the place where certain things are done, . . . and it is not looked upon as a group which God has called into existence to do something."[2]

I think that is well said. All too often the church is viewed as *passive* in its relationship to the world and in its own life. In practical terms, as we have observed, this often adds up to its becoming a religious cushion for the comfort of its shaky members. But De Ridder insists in his book *Discipling the Nations* that the church should be seen as "a commissioned church" with a responsibility to do something to bring in the harvest of non-Christians from the field of the world.[3]

What we are calling for is a rethinking of the Great

---

[1] Belgic Confession, Art. XXIX; Westminster Confession, Art. XXV.
[2] Richard De Ridder, *Discipling the Nations* (Grand Rapids: Baker, 1971), p. 213.
[3] Ibid.

Commission, to read it so as to see that it is defining the church in most radical terms. The missionary mandate is not simply an imperative requiring the church to send missionaries into the harvest field. It certainly is that. But the entire church is a "sent church," a commissioned body that is itself involved in the harvesting task.

The form of the Great Commission recorded in Matthew reads,

> Then Jesus came to them and said, "All authority is given to me in heaven and earth. Therefore while going, make disciples of all the nations, baptizing them into the name of the Father, and of the Son and of the Holy Spirit, and teaching them to observe all things that I have commanded you, and certainly I will be with you all the days to the end of the age" (Matt. 28:18–20 MILLER).

The popular understanding of the Lord's missionary mandate is simply that it calls the church to send out missionaries to distant places. Clearly, that is inherent in the task given us, but this is not all that is implied. What is expressed in Jesus' words is really a commissioning of the whole new people of God. It is the emphatic demand of the risen Lord placed on His people as a whole, and it has reference to the values, priorities, habits, and programs of every member of every congregation. In a word, it means that we are *all* commissioned by the Lord in the Great Commission.

A THREEFOLD COMMISSION

Let us look at the leading features of the Great Commission more closely to test this conclusion and to spell out its meaning in concrete ways. It contains first an Enthronement Proclamation, then a Task Commanded and Defined, and finally a Promise of Power. Since the Enthronement Proclamation and the Promise of Power are closely related, we will treat them as one and afterward discuss the Task Demanded and Defined.

First, the amazing Enthronement Proclamation. The risen

Lord announces in verse 18 that all authority in heaven and earth has been given to Him.[4] In this proclamation Jesus is declaring that a brand new day has dawned, and the cause of that new day is His victory over sin, death, and the devil through His crucifixion and resurrection. This has led the Father to exalt Him to a new enthroned position with all rule and authority given to Him. He has become King of kings and Lord of lords.

The background passage for this proclamation of Jesus is found in Daniel 7, where "a son of Man" receives universal and eternal rule from "the Ancient of Days." In Daniel we learn that the one who draws near to the throne of the Ancient of Days is not a cruel, bestial ruler, but a humane person who brings in a just and kindly rule. This one receives from the Ancient of Days unlimited "authority, glory and sovereign power" (Dan. 7:14). The reach of His authority is universal, and it requires all to surrender in worship to Him. The passage also declares that His kingdom, unlike the bestial kingdoms, is indestructible and eternal. It is virtually a song of praise: "His dominion is an everlasting dominion that will not pass away, and his kingdom is one that will never be destroyed" (v. 14 MILLER).

Jesus, now risen from the dead, is saying in His enthronement proclamation that Daniel 7 has been fulfilled in its first stage. Jesus, the Son of Man, is now on the throne. He is the King of the nations. Jesus is declaring in no uncertain terms that He is Lord of the harvest and that His grand redemptive purpose is to bring into the barn of salvation all the chosen people of God from the nations of the earth.

Legally, Jesus won His victory through His obedient life and death on the cross. By His substitutionary atonement He canceled the debt incurred by our sins and with that legal stroke officially destroyed Satan's authority over the nations. As long as there was no efficacious atonement for sin, the nations stood under God's curse and the condemning authority of Satan as legal accuser. But with Christ's assuming human nature and undergoing a vicarious death for sinners, Satan's

---

[4]See also John 3:35; 5:17–29.

right to condemn transgressors is over. The resurrection signaled the Father's acceptance of His Son's atoning sacrifice and the dethronement of Satan.

Therefore the church now not only has the duty to take the gospel to all the peoples of the earth, but is commissioned to go into *the Lord's harvest* itself. Satan still blinds and binds the nations, but now his work is an illegal guerrilla-style operation. The people are no longer under the authority of the Evil One, but under the authority of the Son of Man, who requires that they submit to His rule speedily, lest He burn them up like chaff at His coming. When the church goes with the gospel, it is not man's will being carried out. The church is out there reporting a divine summons from the throne. The gospel messengers are announcing that the Lord of the harvest is on His way, and now is the hour to surrender to His salvation in faith and repentance.

Positionally, the church does this work as Christ's official representative. His purpose is a grand redemptive one, the forming of a *completed* new people of God out of the rubble of fallen mankind. In the Scriptures this completed church is called "the bride," "the wife of the Lamb," who upon His return will be made perfectly spotless and complete.[5] But the church herself is more than the goal. She is also the vehicle, the instrument, for gathering in the people of God.[6] Christ has no other agency for accomplishing this work. That is why the church is called in this chapter a "commissioned church." It is commissioned to act as Christ's sole representative for carrying the gospel to the nations.[7] Thus the Great Commission assigns the church a task, a missionary purpose, as the means for accomplishing Christ's broader purpose, the ingathering of the whole people of God.[8]

Dynamically, the church is not given an empty commission without divine empowerment. Far from it. In His ascension Christ received the Holy Spirit as the reward for the mighty salvation that He accomplished at Calvary. He has become "a life-giving Spirit" (1 Cor. 15:45 MILLER), a glorified

[5] Ephesians 5:25ff.; Revelation 19–21 MILLER.
[6] Acts 1:8; John 17:20–23; Revelation 22:17.
[7] Luke 24:48–49; John 20:20–23.
[8] Ephesians 4:1–16; 5:25–30; 1:3–23; Revelation 22:17.

Christ imparting "rivers of living water" (John 7:37–39 KJV), "an abounding spring of life" (John 4:10, 14 MILLER), and an abiding missionary presence "to the very end of the age" (Matt. 28:20).

In the form of the Great Commission found in the Gospel of John, Jesus breathes on His disciples as His official representatives in the world (John 20:22). This breathing represents symbolically the coming of the Holy Spirit at Pentecost. At Pentecost Jesus imparted to all the church the witnessing power of His Spirit (Acts 2:17–18). The church is indwelt by a commissioning Spirit, which means that the power for doing the missionary task is Christ dwelling within the people of God. Theirs are the feet that go, the minds that think, the hearers that pray, and the mouths that proclaim. But the sole power for accomplishing the task is not in anything human, institutional, or organizational. It is in Christ.

That is the meaning, then, of Jesus' "Promise of Power" mentioned in verse 20 of Matthew's form of the Great Commission. In verse 18 the Lord announces that all authority in heaven and earth is His. In verse 20 He says that He will be with the disciples "all the days till the end of the age."

There is a connection between the legal enthronement and the dynamic enabling. Because Christ has won the legal victory over sin, death, and Satan and has been enthroned in power, He has the right to commission the church to go with the gospel through His enabling presence. His promise to be with us till the end of the age is no mere pat on the back to say that He will be with us at a distance, with the energizing power supplied by ourselves. No, never! He is saying that in all our work He will be secretly working by His own inward presence in our lives, taking away our fears, giving us love for the lost, enabling us to forgive our enemies and friends, and giving us a fervent trust in the power of the gospel to bring men to faith and eternal life.

It is Jesus' inward enabling that inspires and supports the church through its struggles with the world's hostility and its own sloth. His power will bring in the harvest. When the church acts in obedience to its missionary calling, it does not act alone. But it is not only individual Christians going overseas who have the Holy Spirit given to them. The local church and its members have been given the Spirit as well so that they may gather in those who are outside of Christ. We have both the legal authority to claim the harvest for its Lord and the dynamic authority for bringing the gospel with convincing power. Therefore it is the privilege and duty of each believer to become God's zealous pacesetter in bringing the lost to Christ by every means available.

LEARNING FROM THE PHARISEES

This truth brings us face to face with what appears to be a critical problem: If this awesome authority and invincible, inward power are Christ's gifts to the church of God, why is so little evidence of all this to be found in the local congregation? With something of this tension in view, R. C. Sproul compares many local churches to the company of Pharisees active during Jesus' time on earth. He writes,

> It was the Pharisees who developed the doctrine of "salvation by separation." They were practicing segregationists, believing holiness was achieved by avoiding contact with unclean sinners. No wonder they were scandalized by the behavior of Jesus who dealt with Samaritans, ate dinner with tax collectors, placed His hand upon lepers and ministered to harlots. Our Lord was accused of being a drunkard and a glutton, not because He was overweight or given to intemperance, but because He frequented places where these things were commonplace.[9]

To be sure, this is a familiar issue when we are dealing with the ingrown church, with its false separation. But should this tendency be so dominant in our time? Why is it so prevalent when the authority and the power of Christ are so sovereignly compelling? What is the church missing today?
    The answer is to be found largely in our lack of trust. The passive church member is a person weak in faith. He cannot see the harvest without an eye of faith. That weakness also points out the divine solution to the ingrownness and impotence of the typical local church. We need to recover faith, for

---

[9]"The Christian in the Market Place," in *Tabletalk* (February 1985).

faith is the human side of Christ's authority and empowerment, the vehicle by which He conquers the world out there.
Believing is the way the Spirit of Christ takes over in the
church and makes it a mighty vehicle for outreach to the
perishing human race.

It is no accident that Jesus promised to faith the same
power that He claimed for Himself in the Great Commission. In
the Enthronement Proclamation He declares that all power in
heaven and earth is His. In Mark 9:23 the same Lord also
declares, "Everything is possible for him who believes."[10]
Don't overlook the significance of what Jesus says here. He is
obviously promising to faith what belongs to deity. Only God
is able to find "all things possible" of accomplishment, yet this
is promised to our Christian faith.

How is such a promise to be understood by us in the local
church? Does faith have in itself a magical element—as when
Aladdin rubs the bottle and out pops a genie to do his will?
Not at all. No, what is in view here is an abandonment of our
wills and a claiming of God Himself and the promises He has
made available to us in Christ. In Christ, His promises are ours
in their entirety, and when we pray in faith together, His
divine presence is released in us, overshadowing our work so
that we are enabled to do things that exceed our imagination.
To use the language of John 14:12 once more, we become
"greater works" Christians. As a consequence of our relying on
Christ in this manner, we together as a fellowship of the Spirit
have a unique authority for worship and ministry.

The supreme example of this divine working is recorded
for us in the opening chapters of the Book of Acts. In these
pages we see the apostles and their followers proclaiming the
bodily resurrection of Jesus with unshakable and utterly
convincing faith. They are absolutely sure of Jesus' resurrection and His enthronement at the Father's right hand. Therefore they know that all men are duty-bound to repent of their
sins and to trust in Him as their Savior and Lord. Peter gets
things started by preaching a sermon that leads to the
conversion of three thousand of his hearers on the day of

---

[10] Literally, "all things are able for the one believing" (R. C. H. Lenski).

Pentecost. The bountiful harvest begins. Pacesetters like Stephen and Philip emerge. What makes them pacesetters? Their faith. Luke writes that they are "full of faith and of the Holy Spirit" (Acts 6:5). Consequently, their believing energy spreads the gospel through Jerusalem, then into Judea as a whole, and next into Samaria like the movement of a wind-driven prairie fire.

How do we explain it? We can only account for it as the result of the prayer of the church together, described in Acts 1–4.[11] For every time this "local church" in Jerusalem prays together with "one accord," an unleashing of the divine power follows. Such faith expresses itself in the apostles and the new converts with an openness and a splendid daring that spread faith like contagion (Acts 5–11).

DISCIPLING THE NATIONS

Now we turn to the Task Commanded and Defined and face its magnitude with the eye of faith. Chapter 5 will explain more of the meaning of the command to "go" with the gospel. Here my intention is to put the spotlight on the directive to "disciple all the nations." What is it to "disciple"? Our pacesetting task is not simply to do evangelism to get "decisions," but to do it with intensity, clarity, and thoroughness so that people are brought to faith in Christ and follow Him with heartfelt obedience. Expressed in relationship to the local church, the goal is to add people to the church who are Christians seeking to live in obedience to its Lord.

The Savior also stresses baptism as the initial rite by which new converts separate themselves from the world, put on the badge of discipleship, and testify to their confidence that Jesus is a living Lord. Those who are thus being baptized are to be fully instructed by the church. Nothing less than "all things" that Jesus has taught are to be handed on to those being discipled (v. 19). It would be natural, when we think of the follies that have marred the lives of unwashed sinners, to expect that Jesus would create a class of "also rans" who could

---

[11]Acts 1:13–14; 2:1, 42; 3:1; 4:23ff.

not quite master the practice of discipling. But to take this approach is to minimize the power of Christ in justifying and sanctifying *anyone* who believes in Christ. There are no second-class disciples, because we have a first-class power at work in each one who knows the Lord by faith.

For me personally it was very important to understand this fact. I do not think it is possible for anyone to live in this world without having *some* prejudices toward other kinds of people. For me it was a long, slow process to cleanse my heart of such things. But I had come to see that the command to disciple has a greater sweep than anything I had imagined. I also saw that the saving program of God includes in it large numbers of unwashed "elect" who are not exactly "elite."

A person who had a major part in helping me to see this was Donald McGavran, a pioneer in missions and church growth. When I visited Fuller Seminary in 1968, he succeeded in planting some seeds in my mind that later came to bear unexpected fruit. He generously gave something like an hour of his time while I asked him many questions about church growth and discipleship. Finally I asked him to criticize me frankly—no holds barred—about weaknesses that I might have coming out of my own life and denominational background.

In response Dr. McGavran said with a twinkle in his eye that, as a rule, people in my group were troubled by tendencies toward elitism. He also said that we did not seem to have much practical confidence in the power of the Holy Spirit as Christ's presence, and therefore we tended to be timid. He added that if we divide people culturally into the "washed" and the "unwashed," my group usually went after the washed. The problem with this, he suggested, was that the vast majority of the people in the world are "unwashed." He illustrated what he meant by citing a typical example of a pastor in a poor country overseas. He said, in effect, "If the pastor has a congregation of sixty-five and four of them are professional people, the pastor will aim pretty much his whole sermon at the four."

I accepted his kindly rebuke as the gift of a wise man to me. Eventually the new way I saw the harvest led me to approach the whole process of discipling from a liberated standpoint. The standpoint was that of expectant hope for the salvation of all kinds of people, washed and unwashed, that God might be glorified by the changes wrought by the Spirit's sanctifying power.

The point has been well made by Ralph Winter, the founder of the U.S. Center for World Mission, that the term "nation" does not refer to our modern concept of nations like the United States, Kenya, Germany, or Japan, but to "people groups" that make up human societies. As such it refers to tribes, castes in society, and even looser human associations such as clubs or professional organizations. A "nation" is, stated most broadly, a social group with a perceived sense of self-identity.[12]

Observe also that these "nations" of our text are referred to as "all nations" or "all the nations." That is just another way of saying the whole of mankind. No tribe, no class in society, no religious movement, or race is left out of the Great Commission. To use the imagery of John 3:16, the world of lost sinners is in view, whatever their cultural structure and social order. That means that God loves one's own particular tribe or people subgroup and that it is natural for us to begin our witnessing with our own kind. It is natural for businessmen to reach out with the gospel to businessmen and for homemakers to touch the lives of other homemakers with the good news of the Cross. Likewise, it is a wonderful natural opportunity to take the gospel to members of our own families and to the people in our own neighborhoods.

Still, this insight doesn't make clear the astonishing impact this command would have had on the minds of the Jewish apostles and their fellow disciples in the first century. Consider their mental and religious outlook in respect to the "nations." In the Jewish context, these "nations" are the "outsiders"—tribes and peoples at a distance from the social and religious life of Israel. They are the people who are "far away."[13] Israel is the people of God, the ami, "my people." But

---

[12] Those "nations" that have not yet been reached by the gospel or have access to a viable church Ralph Winter has called "hidden people." See Roberta Winter's *Once More Around Jericho: The Story of the U.S. Center for World Mission* (South Pasadena, Calif.: William Carey, 1978), pp. 223–24.

[13] Isaiah 49:1; Acts 2:39; Ephesians 2:17.

the nations are the goyim, "foreigners to the covenants of the promise" (Eph. 2:12). As outsiders they are ignorant of what counts in matters concerning the knowledge of God, not knowing either the law of Moses or the God of the law. Writing in the *Dictionary of Biblical Theology*, Joseph Pierron and Pierre Grelot put it: "The nations are those who 'do not know God' (the pagans) and those who do not share the life of His people (the foreigners)."[14]

But there is a more serious charge yet against the "nations." They are also the "enemies," a political, military, and religious threat to the integrity of Israel. The power of this awareness is felt in Jonah's intense resistance to God's showing mercy to Nineveh. On the religious side these enemies have taken the glory that belongs to the Lord alone and given it to idols, shameful images that seduce Israel to sin and lead her into paths of destruction. Thus they are no more fit company for the people of God than the lowest outcaste would be for a high-caste Brahmin in India.

Is the picture clear? The Lord of the church is announcing a revolution. Those who are under the wrath of God are now presented as the subjects of His John 3:16 love and the objects of the witness of the church. Through preaching and discipling, those who repent and believe are brought near, even within the walls of an unsegregated church. Awesome!

ACTION STEPS:

1. Memorize John 14:12.
2. Read "Problems with Pea-sized Christianity" in David Bryant's *In the Gap*.
3. For local church officers: Obtain a three-by-five card and write John 14:12 and John 3:16 across the top. Then think of five people whom you know who either frighten you or dislike you or seem strange and "far off" to you. Now write their names below the two texts. Next tape the card to your bathroom mirror and daily pray for their salvation and for an opportunity to present Christ to them.
4. For pastors: Take a month and write down all the names of the people you call upon. Then study the names to see how many of

---

[14]*Dictionary of Biblical Theology* (New York: Seabury, 1973), p. 380.

them are "unwashed" types. You may be surprised how "segre-gated" your ministry is. Now draw up a plan for outreach that involves making at least *one* visit per week to a person radically different from yourself.

READING SHELF

ALLEN, ROLAND. *Missionary Principles*. Grand Rapids: Wm. B. Eerdmans, repr. 1968, pp. 103–134.

BRYANT, DAVID. *In the Gap: What it Means To Be a World Christian*. Madison, Wis.: Inter-Varsity Missions, 1979.

DE RIDDER, RICHARD. *Discipling the Nations*. Grand Rapids: Baker, 1971.

JEREMIAS, JOACHIM. *Jesus' Promise to the Nations*. Trans. S. H. Hooke. London: SCM, 1958.

WAGNER, C. PETER. *On the Crest of the Wave: Becoming a World Christian*. Ventura, Calif.: Regal Books, 1983.

III

UNCOVERING
THE SOURCES
OF MISSIONARY POWER

CHAPTER 5

THE LOCAL CHURCH:
God's Glory
Its Missionary Motive

My question obviously hadn't done anything for my friend's appetite. He put his fork down on the table and replied deliberately, "I find your question hard to answer. How is our church doing? I'd like to say 'just fine,' and there are many reasons for saying that. The congregation has good fellowship, the people love one another as far as I can tell, and things like the budget are going pretty well. We even have an outreach program into the community. But there is something missing. There is nothing driving us to attempt much beyond the ordinary."

My luncheon partner was an elder in a typical suburban congregation, a church where things seemed to be going quite well. But as he groped to express his dissatisfactions, it was clear that life in his congregation could be described as "not much beyond the ordinary."

"We don't have much feel for God's glory moving us, making us take risks to reach the community around us," he concluded. His tone was not condemnatory, but wistful. This elder was hungry for a work of God in the congregation that was not "ordinary." For him, "ordinary" and "glory" were opposites.

In reflecting on his comments, I knew that there can be in

us Christians a lust for excitement that despises the routine work of the church and laboring with the ordinary in the Christian life. Personally I am of the school that holds that effectiveness in ministry is about 90 percent perspiration and 10 percent inspiration. But my friend's definition of "ordinary" and "glory" had a biblical ring. According to the *Theological Dictionary of the New Testament*, the Hebrew word for "glory" has in it the basic idea of being "weighty"— and thus "important" or "striking." It says that "glory" in relationship to God is "that which makes God impressive to man, the force of His self-manifestation."[1]

In other words, the divine glory is that which "strikes" us as something above and beyond the human capacity. It is the *extraordinary* radiance of the divine presence and the supreme exaltation of the divine name, revealed in mighty deeds like the crossing of the Red Sea. The glory of God is the very opposite of the commonplace. Often it is a work of God in man or nature that compels us to stand in awe and silence and to fall on our faces in humility and adoration.

In chapter 2 I told of a young woman named Roberta and her conversion to Christ. Not long after her conversion she contracted meningitis, and then the meningitis apparently activated a brain tumor. One side of her body became paralyzed. A friend and I arrived at her hospital bed around six o'clock on the morning of an emergency operation. Though she could not speak, her face was filled with hope, the light of a confident faith. My friend and I were afraid she was going to die. But it was clear that she was filled with radiant hope.

I smiled and accepted the wonder of her joy. I said, "Roberta, I can tell you believe you are going to get well. I believe it too, with all my heart!" And she did. Later, when she was almost recovered, a doctor asked me, "Where did she get such happiness?"

My answer was, "It comes from God."

At that point in my life and ministry I had begun to develop a working definition of grace and glory. It is this: The

---

[1] Kittel, Gerhard, ed. *Theological Dictionary of the New Testament*, vol. 2, trans. Geoffrey W. Bromiley (Grand Rapids: Wm. B. Eerdmans, 1964), 238.

glory of God is the difference between what we would naturally be or do and what we are enabled to do by God's grace. In her situation, Roberta's natural tendency would have been to complain endlessly. She passed through a period of convulsions followed by meningitis and then underwent brain surgery. I think most of us would have excused her complaining, but instead all I heard from her during this ordeal was praise.

Her radiance in the midst of unbelievable suffering opened up for me a whole new dimension of the Christian encounter with God. Better yet, it was a remarkable example of the encounter of God's glory with a human being, one that filled me with deep, personal assurance that my God is alive and able to do powerful things for His people.

EXTRAORDINARY SERVICE

Luke's account of the life and ministry of Stephen in the Book of Acts offers an even greater illustration of the effects of the divine glory in motivating a life of service to God. In Acts 6, Luke tells us that Stephen was chosen along with six other men to administer the food distribution for the church. He was selected by the congregation because he was an authentic pacesetter in the matter of faith. Luke characterized him as "a man full of faith and of the Holy Spirit," with faith being the conscious expression of the Spirit's indwelling his life (Acts 6:5; cf. 6:3). This quality of faith makes Stephen God's change agent in the New Testament church, evangelist in the Jerusalem community, ardent teacher and defender of the church, and finally the first martyr mentioned in the Book of Acts.

There is almost nothing about Stephen's life and work that can be explained by ordinary causes. Grace is powerfully at work, enabling him to do the following:

1. Have a part in the evangelization of a group highly resistant to the gospel—the priests (Acts 4:1–21).
2. Do wonders and miraculous signs among the people (Acts 6:8).
3. Refute his opponents with remarkable wisdom (Acts 6:9–10).

4. Perceive and teach the spiritual nature of the "temple" (Acts 6:13; 7:47–50).
5. Pass through the trial of the Sanhedrin with his face "like the face of an angel" (Acts 6:7–15).
6. Forgive his murderers with Christlike compassion (Acts 7:59–60).

It is clear that the motivational root of Stephen's joy and his capacity to endure evil lie in his awareness of God's glory. His meditation on the divine honor and majesty had been deep and thoroughgoing. He begins his address to the Jewish senate by speaking of God as "the God of glory," then moves through Israel's inglorious history of idol worship to the tabernacle in the wilderness as the symbol of the divine glory. Having rebuked the members of the Sanhedrin for their "stiff-necked" refusal to honor God, he "looked up to heaven and saw the glory of God, and Jesus standing at the right hand of God" (Acts 7:55).

Notice that Stephen's grip on divine things does not stand still. In a comparatively short time, he moves from a servant of tables to powerful preacher and from preacher to martyr, with a martyrdom characterized by what Peter calls "a glorious joy" (1 Peter 1:8). His critique of the Jewish leaders also centers on God's glory. He is profoundly grieved and angered at their lack of true concern for the glory of God. In his view they have been overly impressed by the external temple, the building, and assumed that the God of glory was bound to the temple almost as though Israel owned God—the opposite of the relationship between God and His people that we discussed in chapter 3. It is this perversion of the self-centered temple worship that Stephen so vehemently denounces. For God, he insists, "does not live in houses made by men," but fills heaven and earth with His majesty (Acts 7:48).

The testimony of a Roberta Peace or a Stephen can be minimized by the thought that "people in our congregation could never be like that." Such an outlook could, of course, be humility based on accurate self-knowledge; but it could also be a deep-seated refusal to yield to the transforming grace of God which is powerful to release us from our fear and bondage.

CHOSEN FOR PRAISE

To get to the heart of this motivational issue, let us return to 1 Peter 2, which we considered in chapter 3. We saw there that the church had three qualities: it was God-owned, God-accepted, and God-separated. But there is another quality, and it heads the list mentioned in verse 9. It reads, ". . . but you are a *chosen* people. . . . " So the people of God were sovereignly chosen by Him for glory—to show forth His "praises." But praises for what? This glorying is not by a complacent religious elite congratulating God for having the wisdom to choose such decent people. Instead, it is praise from those who *know* they were delivered from "darkness"—who once were no people, but now are sensitively aware they are the people of God solely by the power of His grace.

In plain talk, this glorying in God is by those who were the bad and the ugly, the enemies and the aliens who are filled with praise because God's mercy has changed all this. They are not inherently extraordinary, but are worse than ordinary. They are "darkness." Now, however, they have a new motivational compulsion: thankfulness for the difference between what they once were and did and what they now are and do by virtue of God's transforming life working in their souls. They shine with a radiance of gratitude based on God's sovereign call of grace.

The Petrine logic is this: Any believer who knows what he once was and has now become by grace will shine with a "glorious joy."

It was this lack of "glorious joy" in his church that motivated the elder whom I mentioned at the beginning of this chapter. From his perspective the church and its worship seemed to have little in it that could not be explained as the result of human effort and planning. In such a congregation one does not have much *present* sense of deliverance of anyone from real things like an uncontrollable temper, runaway sexual lust, or embittered family relationships. Of course, the language of glory is still in the liturgy of the ingrown church, but it is often there as a faded reality, like the halo above a saint's head in a very old painting, with the gold tarnished by time and forgetfulness.

The Lord's Prayer, for example, has in it a magnificent climax that derives from early church tradition: "For thine is the kingdom, the power, and the glory." But is this magnificent language really descriptive of anything that happened in worship Sunday morning? Is it describing the motivational impulse of a living congregation? Not usually.

Regretfully I conclude that the most fundamental lack in the inward-looking congregation is its loss of touch with the motivational power of the divine glory at work in the church and the world. There is not much among us that is "weighty"—that "makes God impressive to man." Our inward inspiration for doing God's missionary will is thin indeed.

How can this be corrected?

FOUR STEPS TO RENEWAL

Ultimately renewal lies in God's hands. He must pour forth His Spirit as a cleansing presence or we shall not be brought to live for His glory. Nonetheless, what we do in the church is supremely important, because to purpose to live for His glory and to do what we can to promote it in the church and the world is to please God and to lead to the unleashing of His Spirit in our time. So I commend to you four steps that I believe will help you as a pastor or other church officer to move forward this work of renewal in your congregation.

1. *Develop an openness to God's vision for the local church.* It is virtually impossible to recover missionary life and motivation if the leaders and the members of the congregation accept the status quo as normal. In many congregations, for instance, worship is slightly melancholy: the hymns are stately and melancholy, the pastoral prayer is lofty in biblical diction but melancholy, and the sermon as a whole is also melancholy in tone, relieved only by a few happy spots. Even the greeting of one another after the service may be friendly but subdued.

Is this the "inexpressible and glorious joy" of which Peter spoke? Hardly. Many times I have participated in worship services that could have been moved to the local funeral home and been entirely appropriate.

For this reason it is an important step forward in the local church whenever the pastor or other leaders begin to ask questions about the routine of worship. Questions that need to be asked include: How does God see us as we worship together? Is He delighted because, to use the language of Psalm 22, He is being "enthroned on the praises" of His people? Does our worship reveal a growing consciousness among us of the darkness from which we were redeemed? Do we have overflowing thankfulness because a holy God has called us to be His dear children and made us the friends of His own heart?

It will help us and our congregations to engage in healthy self-criticism by studying the life and ministry of Stephen in Acts 6 and 7. Imagine what this pacesetter might say if he came to our churches one Sunday morning. Do you think he would praise you for being sold out with missionary zeal for the sake of the divine glory? Would he say to the Sunday school teachers, "It is wonderful the way you visit the children in their homes during the week and strive for their salvation in prayer?" Would he commend the deacons, "Fellow deacons, I honor you for the way you glorify the Father by pouring out your lives and substance for the poor"? Would he say to the pastor, "Pastor, I can see your face is as radiant as that of an angel as you preach the glory of Christ"? Could he tell the elders, "Brothers, your zeal for spreading the gospel is known throughout the whole region"?

In all this questioning there should be no intention of attacking or hurting anyone. Instead, the purpose is to recover biblical objectivity about the church, to see ourselves more as God sees us. It means that we must learn increasingly to acquire our concept of the church from Scripture and not accept man's commonplace in life and worship as though it were God's normal. What will emerge from such reflection, I believe, will be a vision of the church and its worship as a doxological fellowship, with praise leading the members of the church to go forth boldly with the gospel into the world. Whether it is a new car or a new VCR, people tend to share what they enjoy. If we have glorious joy in worship, we will want to hand it on.

2. *Work to develop an honesty about your sins and weaknesses that leads to change.* To question the prevailing

patterns in a church, though, is not the same thing as to change. Real change can only come as we become convicted by God that the absence of exalted praise and joy is a serious matter—perhaps in God's eyes as bad as committing a sin like adultery. Though I am not able to express my feeling about it fully in words, I believe that faith as a divine power always begins with a recovery of honesty about ourselves in relationship to God. And what is the honest truth about the person seeking to be God's pacesetter in His church? The answer is that I am not naturally surrendered to Christ's will and fully dedicated to living for His praise. I am instinctively a doer. And without Christ's intervention, my first interest is in getting things done in the church and receiving human approval for these accomplishments.

But more than once God has used a stirring example from the life of a more normal Christian leader to arouse me to the truth about my indifference to His glory. That's why I enjoy reading the autobiographies and biographies of Christian leaders of the past. One life that always convicts me is that of Henry Martyn, nineteenth-century missionary to the Muslims of Persia. For instance, at one point a Muslim scholar attempted to comfort Martyn at a time when many Christians were being persecuted by Muslims. He told Martyn a story: "Prince Abbas had killed so many Christians that Christ from the fourth heaven took hold of Mahomet's skirt to entreat him to desist."

The look on Martyn's face upon hearing this fable was one of intense distress. The astonished Muslim asked why.

Martyn replied, "I could not endure existence if Jesus was not glorified; it would be hell to me if He were to be always thus dishonored."[2] For Martyn the very idea of Christ kneeling before Mahomet, a man, made life a hell for him. He knew that the sole reason for his existence was the glory of Christ; he knew no other motivational compulsion in his life.

What troubles me is the realization of how often I have preached without Henry Martyn's motivation. I really do not come to every message with the thought that it will be hell for

---

[2]Constance E. Padwick, Henry Martyn, Confessor of the Faith (New York: Doran, 1922), p. 146.

me if Jesus is not glorified in my proclamation of the Word. Probably many sensitive pastors would agree that our prevailing burden as pastors has often not been to declare fully the absolute supremacy of Jesus Christ ceaselessly until every man has come to live for His glory. And many church members do not seem to come to church on Sunday with strong intent to meet with Christ and be transformed in motivation and values by His glory. So honesty requires us to begin where we are, to confess forthrightly that we have sinned and fallen short of the divine glory.

Such honesty, if it is to bring change, suggests that we tell a Christian friend that we would really like to be a pacesetter for God, but are hung up by religious activism or by a love of our own reputation and a desire for human approval. We must ask that friend to pray that we would really begin to understand what it is to live exclusively for Christ's honor and to experience the freedom and power of a life surrendered daily to His missionary will.

3. *Personalize your relationship with Christ.* The third step is to personalize the biblical teaching about Christ's atoning death for people in "darkness," His subsequent exaltation by resurrection and ascension, and the giving of the Great Commission. I must see that the risen Lord has told me personally to go and disciple the nations for His glory. He also assures me that the power for doing this issues from the majesty of His authority. To accomplish His missionary will, Christ also gives me His Spirit as the enabling power for taking the gospel to all the nations.

So, in my serving for His glory, I must always trust that I am cooperating with Christ, the primary Worker, a fact frequently forgotten by me and other leaders in the local church. The Book of Acts spells it out for me. In my working, I am participating personally in the higher working, the "acts," of the risen Lord.

We must cultivate a faith-consciousness of this New Testament vision. I must see the Son of Man enthroned at the Father's right hand with all power and glory. My Jesus raises His mighty sceptre and speaks, with the result that multitudes come flocking to Him from the ends of the earth. Or, to use the image of 2 Corinthians 2, He is the conquering General, leading all nations captive by faith to His will and destroying all who resist the offer of grace while working through the agency of preachers and witnesses like me. It is my proclamation of the gospel that is His message of life to those who believe and of death to those who reject it.

It is the personalizing of the glory of Christ that motivated Stephen's unflinching courage and made him a compassionate but effective confronter of his hearers. Knowing that Christ stands behind him, Stephen has no fear whatever of those who stand before him. Man and his stones mean little to him. He is caught up in the vision of the glory of the transcendent Christ. Just before the stones begin to fly at him, he says, "Look, . . . I see heaven opened and the Son of Man standing at the right hand of God" (Acts 7:56). Supported by such loving authority, he joyfully accepts his martyrdom as a privilege, an opportunity for showing forth the glory of his own precious Lord. The missionary consequences were great, for doubtless from this time forward Saul, the persecutor, had a troubled conscience, a development that prepared the way for his meeting with the Sovereign Conqueror on the Damascus Road.

The value of being thus able to personalize our relationship to Christ is highly important. But for many Christian leaders and church members, this is not easy. I have found that few church leaders are really motivated by love for the glory of God if they lack assurance that God loves them. For example, a devout Charles Wesley tried to get near to God by all kinds of good works and religious exercises, and he was angered when Peter Boehler told him this was a spurning of grace. Wesley said, "What, are not my endeavors a sufficient ground of hope? Would he rob me of my endeavors? I have nothing else to trust to."[3]

Shortly afterward Wesley turned to Martin Luther's commentary on Galatians and read in the comments on the second chapter that the Christian life consists in "personal

---

[3] Cited in A. Skevington Wood, *The Inextinguishable Blaze: Spiritual Renewal and Advance in the Eighteenth Century* (Grand Rapids: Wm. B. Eerdmans, 1960), p. 111.

pronouns." He discovered that Christ "loved me and gave Himself for me." [4] Abandoning trust in his own "endeavors" and placing all his confidence in Christ's merits, Wesley was speedily assured of God's love for him as a person, convinced that Christ had died for him personally. Out of this personal knowledge of Christ issued Wesley's powerful compulsion to take the gospel to the world.

4. *Commit yourself to express God's glory in every part of your life and service.* We have seen that to glorify God requires openness in discovering God's vision of the normal local church, honesty in seeking change where we do not measure up to that norm, and a personalizing of our whole relationship to God's grace and glory. Now we come to the final and climactic issue, the need for the godly servants of Christ to commit themselves practically to glorifying God in all spheres of life and ministry.

We have seen that to glorify God concerns focusing on what is weighty, important, or striking about Him. But it is also to publicize or *express* the wonder of His person and works. This expression is tied in with the essential trinitarian nature of God, for it is the nature of the Father to express Himself in love to the Son and the Son to express Himself in love to the Father. The story of redemptive history is really the record of the expression of this love of the Father and the Son for one another and their desire to share their community of love with the redeemed community.

This idea was in my head for a long time before it came to have much power in my life as a person and a pastor. For instance, I had drawn the focus on "glorified joy" (1 Peter 1:8) from Jonathan Edwards's *Treatise on Religious Affections*, by 1960. The beauty of a life lived for the glory of God, with the accent on deliverance from darkness into marvelous light, I had met in Edwards's *Personal Narrative* even earlier. But unfortunately, the power of it did not get turned on for my life and ministry. Again, the issue is God Himself: we cannot have something unless God gives it to us.

But by His grace I found a "glorified joy" come into my

---

[4] Ibid., p. 109.

life once I committed myself to express His glory in every part of life and to act with a view to honoring Him. Doubtless I did this with substantial imperfections, but I did launch forth. When my wife and I decided to take troubled people into our home in the early 1970s, I promised to give God the glory for any changes He made in their lives. In January 1973, when we were thinking about beginning New Life Church, we held a "New Life Meeting" in our home. At this meeting some of those who had lived with us told more than forty guests how Christ had changed their lives. The joy of those testimonies to Christ's changing power was so great that it set a whole style of worship for the church subsequently brought into being by the Holy Spirit.

As my repentance deepened, my own part in public worship had more freedom in it, more God-consciousness, and less people-consciousness. This was especially true of my prayers during and after the Sunday worship. Certainly something intrusive was being put into me from outside, something not of me or any man as I prayed and praised God for the glory of Christ. As my spirit more and more celebrated the power of the resurrected Lord, and as my faltering lips cried out for mercy from the Father, I began to meet God in a new way in worship, and so did other people. I have been told that some people were converted through my praying on Sundays. Certainly that is God's grace, because by nature I am not all that enthusiastic about praying. Until about 1970 my pastoral prayers were strictly of a formal kind, forgotten five minutes after they were offered. But in answer to prayer I began to learn a few of the ABCs of speaking to the Father, much to my surprise.

So if we wish to see our congregations renewed, we should express the glory of God in our prayers when we pray on Sunday morning. I am not talking about anything strained, unnatural, or in poor taste, but simple sincerity in holding forth the wonder of Christ's love, the power of His grace to change us, and importunate intercession. I suggest that you pray ahead of time for your pastoral prayer on Sunday. Put thought into it and then ask God for grace just to stand with the people and express in a simple language of love the honor that is due to the heavenly Father. Remember: our whole aim in prayer is to meet with God, and there is no more renewing thing for us and the congregation than to be confronted by His person in a few minutes of holy praise and intercession.

GROWTH IN COURAGE

One of the practical fruits of my commitment to express Christ's glory through life and worship was a growth in courage. It was about this time that Stephen's example from Acts 6 and 7 began to convict me of sin and to help me deepen my repentance, and the deeper the repentance, the less afraid of people I became. I was freed to express love to them in a new way, and to be more concerned for their welfare than for my own cushioning and safety as a pastor. As a result I became much more of a confronter of people in the church. Whether or not it was compassionate confrontation, I began to face many people in my preaching, counseling, and disciplining with the importance of a holy life lived to the glory of God.

As the history of New Life Church unfolded and the church grew rapidly, I think in reflection that much of my contribution lay right here. I was surprised at how, lacking exhortation and admonition, a newborn, renewal church like ours can drift into complacency. First, my own pride was always ready to rear its ugly head. Failure is not easy to live with, but neither is success, and pride can flourish when things go well. Second, the members of our church again and again began to show all the signs of the introverted congregation. Counterculture people did not want to welcome new middle-class members. Or zealous deacons saw evangelistic types as uncaring and irrelevant, and evangelistic types suspected deacons of neglecting the gospel for the sake of social concern. Sometimes in worship all of us sank together into dullness and metronome sameness.

One of the early co-pastors, Ronald Lutz, worked a great deal on the organization of the life of the church. He also labored with me in my chief role, as an affirmer of the brothers and sisters and as a confronter of my sins and theirs. Our being willing to do this impossible work was in itself an expression of God's glory. For me it is natural to avoid conflicts. But through mutual admonition God prospered our work with a

peace and a unity that would have been impossible from a
human point of view. For only Christ could have used this
combination of love and correction to give us almost fourteen
years of remarkable growth, unity, and peace.

Ron and I both feel very ordinary as people, but we serve
an extraordinary Christ who has in grace been pleased to
express Himself through us. The glory is His. The weaknesses
are ours.

ACTION STEPS:

1. Reflect on the following statements on the glory of God:

   "The glory of God is the very opposite of the
   commonplace."

   "The glory of God is the difference between what we
   would naturally be or do and what we are enabled to
   do by God's grace."

2. Write your own definition of the glory of God.
3. Ask yourself the following questions about your definition:
   Is it biblical? Is it concrete? Does it communicate anything to
   others? Has it influenced your life in a basic way?
4. Using the four steps mentioned in this chapter, develop a plan for
   making the glory of God the motivational power for your life and
   ministry. Include in your plan an honest facing of competing
   motivations in your life.

READING SHELF

EDWARDS, JONATHAN. "Personal Narrative," *The Works of Jonathan Edwards*, 2 vols. London: Banner of Truth Trust, 1965.

ELLIOT, ELISABETH. *Through Gates of Splendor*. New York: Harper
Brothers, 1957.

HOWARD, DAVID M. *Declare His Glory*. Downers Grove, Ill.:
InterVarsity, 1977.

ORTIZ, JUAN CARLOS. "The Language of the Kingdom," *Disciple*.
Carol Stream, Ill.: Creation House, 1975.

OWEN, JOHN. *The Glory of Christ*. Vol. 1, *The Works of John Owen*.
London: Banner of Truth Trust, repr. 1965.

CHAPTER 6

THE WELCOMING LOCAL CHURCH

A case has been made for regarding the normal local congregation as a "commissioned" church, a glory-fellowship aggressively taking the gospel to the world. But how does this work at the practical level of congregational life? What does the commissioned church do that is different from what is done in the stagnated, passive congregation?

The answer is essentially that the commissioned church is *hospitable*. It aggressively and joyfully seeks out the unchurched, laboring to welcome them into the church as members of the body of Christ. Its leaders self-consciously reject a "Christian clubhouse" atmosphere and devote themselves to developing in the congregation an open face to the community and the world beyond. The local leaders model a welcoming lifestyle and seek to mobilize others to do the same.

For the pacesetting church leader, it is of utmost importance to see that this vision of the welcoming church is God's norm for the congregation, for we will find great resistance in the local church to God's open-door policy. I believe that it is often easier to inspire Christian people to go overseas as "missionaries" than it is to get them to welcome their neighbors into their lives.

Therefore we ourselves need to be captured by God's

vision of the New Testament church in its resurrection reality. In Acts 2 we encounter God's new creation, the beginning of the new people of God. Standing just beyond the congregation's empty tomb, awed by the Spirit's presence, they are filled with mutual love and are witnessing through hospitality to the community. This Christ-centered church, in its welcoming openness to the unsaved, is God's permanent model for the age of faith.

Regrettably, it is characteristic of our time that local church leaders too often accept the passive church model as normative. The model of the church in Jerusalem, Antioch, or Thessalonica is admired from a distance, but there is little enthusiasm for cultivating a similar openness to the world. The leadership in the typical introverted church is tired, and so are the people. There is simply not enough zeal for Christ working in their hearts to compel them to open their homes to the unchurched.

Interestingly, I believe that many congregations are so dulled to the biblical norm of the welcoming church that the officers and members assume that they are much more welcoming than they actually are.

A FRIENDLY CHURCH?

About ten years ago I was invited to lead a preaching crusade in a church in one of Texas's major cities. When Rose Marie and I arrived, we were impressed by the friendliness of the members toward us. Located in a suburban area, they seemed to have the friendly manner of typical American suburbanites. In fact, they themselves stressed that they were "a friendly church that welcomes visitors."

As we moved among the people, we began to hear this we-are-a-friendly-church refrain again and again. It sounded in our ears enough to make us wonder: Why do both officers and church members protest so much about their friendliness? Are they seeking reassurance because of self-doubts?

The members were also quick to point out many of the excellent features of the congregation. They noted that the pastor was a faithful man who loved the people. They seemed to be of one mind that he preached "good sermons that were often outstanding." The men of the church were turning out almost twenty strong every morning at six o'clock to pray for the evangelistic meetings taking place each evening. Their prayers were fervent and sincere. Who would not be impressed by all this?

But there were some hard facts about the congregation that puzzled the leaders and members of the church. The congregation had an official membership list of about three hundred, and two years ago that number of people were attending Sunday morning worship. But by this time the attendance was down to two hundred and still declining.

Members made comments like the following:

"Ninety-five percent of the visitors to our Sunday services don't return for a second visit."

"People here aren't too committed. You can't get them to do much. It's really discouraging."

"Over the past two years church attendance keeps going down, and it makes you feel that something is really wrong with us and you don't know what."

To probe the matter, I kept asking questions about the friendliness of the church and its welcoming tone. The women of the congregation especially insisted that they were "one of the friendliest churches in the community." To find out if this friendliness had any substance in it, I interviewed a recent visitor to one of their Sunday morning services. This woman told me, "I had no trouble at all in making it to the door without a *single* person greeting me—except the pastor."

The visitor summed up the problem. "I noticed that they gathered in little groups to greet their friends. They are friendly to each other and think that means they are also friendly to visitors."

A burly deacon in the church confirmed this report when I asked him about the church's decline. He said, "We all say we are puzzled by our slide in church attendance and membership. We all feel we should be growing. We get frequent visitors, and there are many unchurched homes all around us. But our problem is that we don't mean business for God. We give only a halfhearted welcome to visitors. Actually **we are expecting the pastor to do all the real work of** welcoming. He's a hard worker, and he carries the rest of us on his shoulders."

The deacon was right. The members were passive, not active in welcoming people. If they happened to be standing next to a visitor after the services, they would shake hands, but they did not cover any distance to do this, and as far as I could tell no one was inviting guests to come to their homes for lunch or dinner. If we were to compare this body of Christians with those in Acts 2, it would immediately become clear that this Texas congregation lacked intensity of devotion to Christ and His cause. In actuality they saw the Lord's command to go and disciple the nations as applying almost exclusively to religious professionals like pastors, missionaries, and evangelists. The Great Commission did not come to their minds as a total demand upon their lives by a sovereign Master, but a piece of good advice to be heeded or ignored as they saw fit. And most of the time they saw fit to ignore it.

THE GREAT AMERICAN CHURCH TRAGEDY

I was standing in the midst of the Great American Church Tragedy. That tragedy is the local church with an abundance of resources and spiritual gifts held back by unbelieving apathy and blinded by the strange notion that the work of missionary outreach is the domain of a few highly trained leaders.

The congregation had in it many evidences of maturity— a mature pastor and elders, a well-run Sunday school, and a fellowship of godly older women. Unfortunately, these positive qualities helped disguise the fact that this congregation was sick unto death. The decline in church attendance was a public registering of the chilling complacency that was seeping into the lives of more and more of the members. Obviously many folks in the church were already so iced over that they preferred to sleep in on Sunday mornings. Generally even the most active members of the church appeared to do little real witnessing. They had lost touch with the whole idea of the lostness of their neighbors and friends and had more of a fear of strangers than anything else.

As I struggled to get hold of the basic problem in this congregation, it became clear that the church needed thorough-going repentance. But repentance for what?

The people had grown cold toward God, and the peril of the lost no longer touched apathetic hearts. They needed to humble themselves and turn to God for grace to love Him and the strangers who were all around them.

But the change needed to go even deeper than this, because their coldness was rooted in wrong theology and a related misunderstanding of the Great Commission. Theologically they had been heavily influenced by the biblical teaching on election. Nothing wrong with that—it is there in the Bible. Yet it had been understood in a one-sided manner that had canceled out God's character as a "welcoming God," a hospitable Father who loves to take repentant sinners of all kinds into His loving arms. These Christians had understood God's sovereignty to mean that if people were going to be saved, they would be saved no matter what anyone did or didn't do. This is not biblical teaching, but something closer to the Muslim doctrine of kismet, impersonal fate. This misunderstanding had set in cement their indifference to the lost. It was an awesome theological justification for slothful disobedience to the will of the Lord.

This doctrine of fatalism was coupled with a misunderstanding of the Great Commission.[1] As I talked with the officers and members of the congregation, it became clear to me that they understood that the "go" of the Great Commission applied primarily and almost exclusively to the pastor and to other specially trained people like evangelists and "foreign missionaries." I believe it is this mistaken view of the Great Commission that accounts for the loss of the missionary life of the local church.

To help bring this Texas congregation to repentance, I called them back to the God of the Scriptures and the words of the Great Commission, especially focusing on the significance of Jesus' word "go." I taught the men from the Book of Hebrews to build their faith as we met at six o'clock each

---

[1] For what follows, see Roland Allen, Missionary Principles (Grand Rapids: Wm. B. Eerdmans, repr. 1968), pp. 36–44; and James A. Scherer, Missionary, Go Home! A Reappraisal of the Christian World Mission (Englewood Cliffs, N.J.: Prentice-Hall, 1964), pp. 45–52. I am indebted to Allen and Scherer for bringing into sharp focus how the professionalizing of evangelism and missions has led to complacency in the local church.

morning. I stressed that God presents Himself to our faith as a hospitable God, a welcoming God through Christ's permanent, heavenly intercession. What we do, then, in our own hospitality is simply to mirror in our relationships the openness and access that we have already experienced with our Father. Our evangelism takes off from this focal point. By faith we open our homes and hearts to others just as God has opened His welcoming salvation to us.

My wife and I taught the older women the same principles at the ten o'clock hour later in the morning. This time we used the Epistle to the Romans. We underscored the truth that God is a God of hope. We did not minimize what Romans says about the wrath of God, but we put the spotlight on the Pauline teaching that God is a God of hope, a welcoming God, who invites us to welcome one another just as Christ welcomed us (Rom. 15:7, 13).

As we stressed God's nature as a welcoming God of grace, we also taught them that each one of us is called to "go" with the gospel—not just the pastor and the church leaders. We labored on this point especially with the church officers. Our whole burden was to persuade and motivate pacesetters in the church to see that they were duty-bound to rely on the grace of a hospitable God to reach out to the lost.

I think what they heard was a radically different version of the Great Commission. Of course, I do not deny the role of the church in sending out specially trained missionaries to reach those who have never heard the gospel. But I taught these believers that this does not exhaust the meaning of the "go" of the Great Commission. Instead, the primary action of going begins right where we are. It means nothing more or less than going into the harvest field. "Going" means *moving* into the work and doing it aggressively.[2] We might almost say that it means going down right where we are, humbling ourselves by plunging into the work or reaping with those around us, reaching both those who are like us and those who are unlike us.

---

[2]"Going" in Matthew 28:19 is a present participle describing the imperative verb "to disciple." As such it emphasizes the activity of discipling as a vigorous action, an ongoing enterprise.

This humbling side of the Great Commission has been especially highlighted in its Johannine form. Jesus says, "As the Father has sent me, I am sending you."[3] And how did the Father send Jesus, according to the Gospel of John? He sent Him with all authority, but that authority was allied with total humiliation. Jesus conquered all, but He conquered by going down to the depths in order to purchase our salvation.[4]

HUMBLED TO CONQUER

This is our model. We go down in humiliation in order to conquer with the gospel. How beautifully this teaching harmonizes with the stress of Romans on our God as a welcoming God of hope! We go down in humility as we open our lives in hospitality. But why do so few Christians today open their hearts and homes to the non-Christian community? The reason is that they are fearful of being hurt by involvement with others. They do not want the trouble and the risk, the exhaustion that hospitality brings, the struggles with sloth that it requires, and all the rest of the suffering that it entails.

But this fear of the cost of discipleship will disappear if Christian people begin to see how great is God's love in welcoming them to His fatherly heart. As I taught the people in this Texas church and called them to repentance for their wrong view of God and their failure to go with the gospel, I stressed His unconditional love for them, His abundant grace for them despite their disobedience to His will, and the fact that they are now by faith welcomed into His presence. I talked about the power of Christ's atoning sacrifice to take away the veil that separates the sinner from God, so that we may find grace to be His welcoming representatives to the world.

I knew in my heart that there was no power in me to change these people. Left to myself, I am just like them, and perhaps even worse in my coldness. But the preaching of the cross as it is presented in Romans and Hebrews is a mighty, unstoppable power. I think of what it did for men like Luther, John Bunyan, John Wesley, Charles Wesley, George Whitefield,

---

[3] John 20:21; cf. 17:18.
[4] John 1:14; 12:23–26.

and Howell Harris. In his preface to his commentary on Romans, Luther says that the gospel, when received by faith alone, sets people aflame with the power of the Holy Spirit. He writes,

> For faith through the merit of Christ, obtaineth the Holy Spirit, which Spirit doth make us new hearts, *doth exhilarate us, doth excite and inflame our heart,* that it may do those things willingly of love, which the Law commandeth. . . . "[5]

So when God blessed my teaching on grace to turn some hearts to obedience, I was not surprised. That is the way the gospel and the Spirit work. Preach the message of a receiving Father through faith in Christ and in reliance on the Holy Spirit, and we have every reason to expect people to change right along with us. But there is a bit more to it when it comes to application.

This "more" was supplied by one of the deacons in the church. With disarming candor he went to the pastor, humbled himself to work through some personal conflicts between them, and then daringly begged the pastor in words like these:

> Dear pastor, we all love you very much, but you have got to open up and let us know how this decline in church attendance breaks your heart. Let us know how you feel about how we have let you down by giving you all the work to do.

Growing in his knowledge of God's love for him, the pastor received this admonition with humility and did something about it. He got on the telephone and began to call the fading members to the evening meetings. The first two evenings' attendance had been barely thirty-five people, but because of his work on the telephone, by Wednesday the size had nearly doubled. This pastor was humbly aggressive on the telephone. In a broken spirit, he spoke directly from the heart and said how saddened he had been by the lack of response to the evangelism series, and how much he felt he was being left alone in the work. He said plainly, "I am asking you to come to these meetings. Please do it."

---

[5] Cited in Henry Bett, *The Spirit of Methodism* (London: 1937), pp. 21–22.

By Friday evening the church was filling up. There was a heavy thunderstorm right before the meeting at 7:30, but people came anyway. One could see that they were expecting something to happen. It did. A visitor from another church later told me, "You could feel the storm outside, with its electricity, and you could feel a kind of electricity when you began to speak. It was humbling in a mysterious way to be there, as though you knew God was there and could not be stopped from doing what He planned to do to break people down."

After my message on the theme of a welcoming God, I invited the pastor to give his testimony to the congregation and the visitors. There was nothing accusatory or condemnatory in it. It was simply a broken man confessing that he was broken and telling the congregation honestly why he felt they had failed him. In effect, he said with many tears,

> Many times I have asked you to help me in the work and told you how unable I am to do it. Now I want to tell you I cannot go on without your help. We must be a team together, partners before God. My friends in Christ, you know how much I love you, but you are not participating in the work of God. You have not taken me seriously when I have asked you to get involved with me in it. I am not the Holy Spirit. I am only me. I simply cannot go on this way, trying to do my work and yours. I repent of my having failed to insist upon this with you, and I now want to encourage you to see me as I really am, a weak man who desperately needs your help.

A spirit of repentance and revival came upon all of us as the pastor spoke, touched off by his humility and openness with God and the congregation. Though this man probably did not know it, he greatly resembled Christ at that moment. In a real way he was going with the gospel, and in a mysterious manner we were the harvest field. As we listened to him, we all began to break down and weep. Every one of us was convinced of our stubbornness in refusing to bring the gospel to others. It became clear that such a refusal revealed a deep ingratitude to God for His coming to us through the humiliation and death of His Son.

That night about fifty men came forward to rededicate

their lives to serving Christ by active outreach and witness. I believe these pacesetters responded to Christ's welcome with all their hearts. They certainly responded to the pastor with an unprecedented outpouring of love that was not present in the church before that evening's work.

The results of the Spirit's activity were highly encouraging in the weeks and months that followed. The congregation had a quickened vision of the priority of aggressively welcoming visitors to the church services, and this welcoming was fueled by a new confidence in Christ's welcoming of each church member through His grace. The evangelism program of the church was reorganized and the work was intensified. More members became involved in the work of the ministry. Before long, there were a number of professions of faith in Christ, and the church stopped declining and began to grow. More time was spent in corporate prayer to seek God's blessing on the ministry.

THE ELEMENTS OF NEW LIFE

Looking back, I am deeply grateful to Christ for what He did in this church. But I can also see how I would do more today to try to reorient the life of such a church more thoroughly. Here are some of the elements I would like to see brought into a local church as permanent features of its life.

1. I would stress to the pacesetting pastor the supreme importance of preaching the gospel clearly and boldly, and his need to recruit people to pray regularly that this might take place. Preaching in the United States and elsewhere in the modern world tends to be strongly moralistic and legalistic rather than Christ-centered. Often the emphasis is on doing, without a foundation being laid in the grace of a God who welcomes sinners to Himself unconditionally. In other words, the pastor can unintentionally short-circuit the welcoming process by depressing the people with joyless preaching that concentrates on doing things rather than relying on Christ for help to obey the will of God.

2. I would emphasize the importance of orienting the worship service around God's welcoming person and grace. I

would be much more careful to choose singable hymns that focus on Christ's resurrection and ascension, the basis of God's welcome to us. I would not hesitate to use songs and music that focus on our sins, but I would do so to bring people to an honest appreciation of divine grace in its surpassing abundance. I would emphasize testimonies of church members and new converts to make all aware that God's gospel of grace is active and changing people by faith in their midst. Such a service style builds pacesetting faith, and faith works by love and awakens hope and expectancy of God's further working.

3. I would labor to make every organization in the church develop what our congregation calls an "outward face" toward the world. The deacons should plan their work so as to get involved with the forgotten people of the community: the elderly in nursing homes, the sick, the unemployed, the people in prisons, and the dying. The elders should not act merely as an official board, but also plan times of shared hospitality to which they invite non-Christian guests. The trustees should take utmost care to see that the church building advertises the joy of salvation by being freshly painted and in good physical condition (especially the nursery). Every effort should be made to convert the Sunday school into a vehicle for welcoming families from the neighborhood, with multiple classes for adults. Perhaps the Sunday school would also be a natural place for a class on hospitality, taught in one quarter of each year.

4. I would develop new programs designed to meet the needs of the community. The church should decide which needs it is most equipped to meet and then pray and organize with a view to meeting these needs. Going with the gospel needs a direction, a planned outlet. Ask yourself what gifts and abilities are resident in the members of the congregation. Then see how these resources harmonize with the needs of people living around you. For example, many churches organize a men's friendship breakfast on Saturday mornings with a special speaker. Others organize fellowship initiatives for medical people or single parents. If you have an abundance of Bible teachers, you can organize Bible studies in the community or increase the number of adult Sunday school classes.

Obviously, all that is being suggested at this juncture could lead the church into an exhausting busyness. But it need not do so if this moving into the work is a shared enterprise undertaken by faith. You will need a continued, strong emphasis on the hospitable character of God and your need for continual repentance and cleansing from your indifference. The very message you proclaim will heal and renew you. As you go and disciple the nations, you will find that your welcoming God constantly enlivens you through the message of grace which you proclaim to others.

ACTION STEPS

1. In one or two sentences summarize the concept of "going" (Matt. 28:1) as expressed in this chapter.

   Do the same for the concept of God as a "welcoming God."

   Do the same for the concept of the "welcoming church."

2. Consider praying the following: "Holy Father, open the eyes of my heart so that I may understand the Great Commission as it applies to my congregation and to my own life. Enable me to become a welcoming person who models by my life your welcome of love to me. In Christ's name."

3. Prayerfully select two people (or two couples) to train as models of hospitality and train them, using chapters 5–10 in my book *Evangelism and Your Church* as a training guide.

4. Propose to your elders or church board the formation of a task force to study groups in your community whom your church has the resources and gifts to reach.

5. Set aside an evening to discuss with the elders or church board how visitors can be more warmly welcomed Sunday mornings. Take this opportunity to introduce what you propose to do by way of training (see above).

READING SHELF

ALDRICH, JOSEPH C. *Life-Style Evangelism: Crossing Traditional Boundaries to Reach the Unbelieving World.* Portland: Mult-nomah Press, 1981.

FALWELL, JERRY. *Capturing a Town for Christ.* Old Tappan, N.J.: Fleming H. Revell, 1973.

MAINS, KAREN B. *Open Heart, Open Home.* Elgin, Ill.: David C. Cook, 1976.

McGINNIS, ALAN LOY. *The Friendship Factor.* Minneapolis: Augsburg, 1979.

MILLER, C. JOHN. *Evangelism and Your Church.* Phillipsburg, N.J.: Presbyterian and Reformed, 1980.

STAFFORD, TIM. *The Friendship Gap.* Downers Grove, Ill.: InterVarsity, 1984.

CHAPTER 7

THE PRAYING
LOCAL CHURCH

As I drove up to the church building in our California city that Wednesday evening, I wasn't surprised to see the parking lot empty. I was usually the first person to arrive for prayer meeting. A few moments later I was arranging chairs and reviewing my thoughts for the evening's Bible study.

But after waiting about ten minutes, I became puzzled. Usually Maria was here by this time, and Tom and Mary, and Brian. Our midweek prayer meeting was never large, but we always had at least a small group turn out. I glanced again at my watch. It was ten to eight! Twenty minutes had gone by and I was still alone. At eight o'clock I went to look at the parking lot. There was not a single car to be seen.

With a sinking feeling, I made my way back to the prayer room. Obviously no one was coming. What had happened? Who killed the prayer meeting?

Several people over the previous year had not exactly helped build it. One brother sometimes argued with me over details of the Bible study. Another probably prayed too long during the prayer time. But as I struggled with questions, I sensed a disturbing answer pushing forward into the light. It was: "You killed the prayer meeting!"

I had killed the prayer meeting? That was an alarming thought. The pastor had done the prayer meeting to death? But if I as pastor had killed the prayer meeting, I did not have a clue as to how and why it had happened.

Turning from this dismal picture, I will share a second scene that has never left me. Ten years later I drove again into a church parking lot, this one belonging to a small country church in Pennsylvania that I was serving as pastor. It was in July 1971, and the lot was filled with cars. So many people were packed into the church basement that you could hardly enter the door or find a place to sit. We had to adjourn to the sanctuary to provide space for all the people.

On that night, four people made professions of faith, lives of believers were changed, and a carload of passing teenagers stopped to see what all the excitement was about at this once sleepy church.

"What's happening, what's going on?" their leader asked. "I've driven by here many times, but I've never seen this kind of action. What's up?"

This teenager was the president of the student council at a local high school, a fine student, and an outstanding athlete—and secretly addicted to drugs. A few weeks later someone sent him some evangelistic literature through the mail, and he surrendered his life to Christ and became active in our prayer meeting.

WHAT MADE THE DIFFERENCE?

What made the difference between the prayer meeting that failed and the one that came alive? The earlier gathering lacked the touch of the power of God. In the second one the King was present, moving, working, and leading. It was His meeting. He had graciously chosen to be present and to glorify Himself by changing us and answering our prayers.

Seen from the human side, people came to the prayer meeting because they expected God to work in their lives. They expected to know God better for having come, and they were convinced that He was ready to answer their prayers. I cannot remember their being disappointed. Each week we heard reports of prayers being answered and lives changed. One thing really brightened up the meetings: it was not unusual for the unconverted people we had prayed for a few weeks before to become Christians and begin to attend the prayer meetings. Sometimes people were converted during the Wednesday meeting itself.

Much of the change, thought was in me and in my view of the Holy Spirit. My understanding of God and His commitment to supply the Holy Spirit was shallow and intellectualistic. I was especially afraid of anything in worship or prayer that might be emotional or what I saw as "spooky." At bottom, it was a matter of trust. I relied heavily—sometimes almost entirely—on my mind as a Christian thinker and on my hard work as a pastor. Prayer and what the apostle Paul calls "the fellowship of the Spirit" were "dispensable supplements" for me as a pastor. What really mattered for me was frequent and regular visiting of people, studying the Bible carefully, preaching biblical truths with contemporary relevance, and often using the media to publicize the programs of our local church. In all this I had a naïve confidence that biblical truths clearly expressed would almost automatically change lives.

Fortunately a second failure eventually did a great deal more to clear the cobwebs from my busy pastoral brain. Elsewhere in this book I have told about it—my humbling struggle with an overwhelming sense of defeat in the spring of 1970, and my subsequent intense study of the promises of God. I still valued clearheaded thinking about the Bible and intense pastoral labor. But I began, haltingly but really, to give up my confidence in any human adequacy and my own abilities. I tried to rely more exclusively on "prayers and the supply of the Spirit" (Phil. 1:18 MILLER) for the power to serve Christ effectively.

Increasingly I saw myself as a desperately needy person, like the man who goes to his friend at midnight and says, "I have nothing" (Luke 11:6). Before this, my problem in praying was that I had something—namely, reliance on myself, my training, my study, and my work. But the man at midnight has no bread for himself or for others. In his total need he forgets all sense of dignity. The standard translations of verse 8 speak of the man's "persistence," but that is hardly what the original language indicates. A better translation would be "shamelessly persistent" or even "shamelessly pushy." Once I began to pray boldly like this man in my hunger for God and His help, He began to impart to me in a new way the presence of the Holy Spirit.

And that is the whole point of this passage that compares bread and food to the Holy Spirit. God promises in Luke 11:13: "If you then, though you are evil, know how to give good gifts to your children, how much more will your Father in heaven give the Holy Spirit to those who ask him!" What came home to me with power is the centrality of the Spirit's working for all of the Christian life and service. In my need I came to appreciate what Herman Bavinck stresses in his excellent essay "The Gift of the Spirit."[1] He says that all the promises of Scripture—for protection, health, daily physical bread, etc.—find their root in the one supreme promise: the commitment of the risen Christ to impart the Holy Spirit as the power source for the church in answer to prayer.

In practice this meant for me that I began to pray for the Spirit's presence to be with almost everything I did. I especially began to pray with "shameless boldness" for His working in our prayer meeting. I also prayed for each person who was likely to come, for anyone who had a part in leading the prayer meeting, and for my own leadership during the prayer time. I asked God to give us His Spirit that we would know how to pray, that our hearts would be surrendered to His missionary will, and that we would leave the prayer meeting freed of guilt and fear and ready to witness fearlessly for Christ. In brief, my plea, based on the promise of the Spirit given in Luke 11:13, was for Him to meet with us and change us into a community of faith working through love. Frequently I asked the Father to visit us with His Spirit to equip us with three things:

1. His self-forgetting love for others,

2. His wisdom for praying specifically and intelligently,

3. His boldness for prayer and risk-taking witness.

---

[1] Herman Bavinck, "The Gift of the Spirit," in Our Reasonable Faith (Grand Rapids: Wm. B. Eerdmans, 1956), pp. 386–403.

TWO KINDS OF PRAYER MEETINGS: MAINTENANCE OR FRONTLINE?

This prayer meeting in Pennsylvania was intended to function as a *frontline* battle station. the earlier meeting in California was largely designed to *maintain* the existing life and ministry of our congregation. Believers came to the earlier meeting to be edified by a Bible study that took up most of the hour and to pray for the internal needs of the church. Expectancy seemed to be at a low ebb among the attenders, evidenced by the fact that none of us bothered to keep a record of prayers offered and answered. I also do not think that Christians came to this prayer meeting expecting to meet God in a life-changing encounter.

By contrast, people came to the frontline prayer meeting to be *changed*. They discovered what Augustine has emphasized, that man's chief need is to fellowship with God, to find fulfillment in Him, and to experience the abiding presence of Jesus (Pss. 27:4; 36:7–9; John 14:18–23; 15:1–10). So they came to be changed, and they were changed because Jesus kept His promise to be wherever two or three gather in His name (Matt. 18:19–20). From Him they received grace to confess and forsake their sins, to be touched with His compassion for the lost, and to go forth to "put feet on their prayers" through witnessing by words and deeds of love.

Speaking of maintenance-style prayer meetings, Steve Harper says bluntly that "they are not really prayer meetings." In his useful little book *Prayer Ministry in the Local Church*, he concludes, "They are usually Bible studies with five minutes of prayer tacked on at the end."[2] Ours in California actually was given to prayer, but its conception and format were designed more to preserve the status quo of the inward-looking church than to break down its rigidities. By contrast, the frontline prayer assembly has a revolutionary purpose. The prayer of those who attend it is summarized in the words "Thy kingdom come." Their Spirit-imparted desire is to see the power of God's kingdom revealed and to see the social

---

[2]*Prayer Ministry in the Local Church* (Grand Rapids: Baker, 1976), p. 45.

segregation of the turned-in church replaced by a welcoming community of faith and love. Such a frontline prayer meeting becomes itself an expression of kingdom power when the following conditions are met:

1. *Faith/expectancy:* A minimum of two or three believers gathered together to devote themselves to prayer and confidently claim Jesus' promise to be present with them (Matt. 18:20; Acts 1:13–14; 2:42).

2. *Oneness of purpose:* A seeking of "agreement" (Matt. 18:19) or "one-mindedness" (Acts 1:14; 2:1; 4:24; Rom. 15:5–6) on key subjects for prayer.

3. *Authority:* A humble but bold claiming of the authority of Jesus' name in making requests of the Father (Matt. 18:20; John 15:16; 16:24).

4. *Commitment:* A surrender to the will of Christ as revealed in the Great Commission, and a willingness to take "risks" in obeying that will (Acts 1–4).

You can see more clearly what this kind of prayer involves in practice when you consider the content and format of a typical frontline prayer meeting. For example, in 1971 one of our prayer meetings might have had the following order and elements in it:

Opening—reading a promise concerning the Holy Spirit from John 7:37–39, singing several "singable" songs exalting Christ, praying for the Spirit's presence;

Testimonies of answers to prayer and thanksgiving, and opportunities to confess sins and claim the Father's forgiveness;

Reading and brief exposition of Matthew 18:19–20 on the nature of corporate prayer;

Agreement and prayer for key subjects—overseas missionaries, preaching of the Word on Sunday, unsaved friends and neighbors, seriously ill people, youth work and Sunday school;

Songs of praise for the answers anticipated;

Dividing up into small groups to pray for felt needs—fears and anxieties, family problems, employment, finances.

This prayer time would usually last almost an hour and a half, but the elders of the Chapel and I would stay around for at least another hour to help people "put feet on their prayers." One purpose of this follow-up time was to guide believers into avenues of service for Christ in the church and community. Later, when New Life Church was born in 1973, this after-period became a "commitment time" for mobilizing deacons for outreach to nursing homes and the poor and for stimulating sluggish Christians to reach out more boldly in witness. With our heads cleared by the evening of prayer, we often came to see much more clearly the needs of the community around us and to seek out spiritual gifts for ministering to these needs.

To build this kind of action-oriented prayer meeting, I personally invited all kinds of people to attend, something that I had not done with the earlier prayer meeting. I told them, "It's the best meeting in the church. Come and expect great things to happen." Those who responded were usually people who felt a need to know God better and were becoming teachable.

In the beginning I was most successful in persuading businessmen to come to pray, since they were often willing to be discipled by me. Eventually I sent almost all my counseling cases to this meeting. Next I zeroed in on the teenagers of the church, made friends with them, and shared with them my excitement over what God was doing Wednesday nights. Soon a dozen teenagers were attending. This was not cheap sales-manship, but persuasion issuing from the Spirit's building in me a biblical vision of the meaning and power of corporate prayer.

By the summer of 1971 I was absolutely convinced of the supreme importance of corporate prayer if the ingrown fellow-ship is to recover New Testament normalcy.[3] I was equally

---

[3] By this time I saw that the premier means by which we claim the power of the Spirit for witness is through the corporate prayer of the church. Striking evidence supporting this conclusion is seen in Peter's transformation after Jesus' resurrection. Before the resurrection he was the man who slept while Jesus prayed. But afterward he is "devoted to prayer" with the other disciples (Acts 1:13–14), and he is filled with extraordinary boldness in his preaching as a consequence of this commitment to corporate prayer (Acts 2:16–41).

convinced that a normal Christian life requires participation in corporate prayer. My earnestness and sincerity in these matters were certainly a gift of God and not arising from myself, but God graciously used His working in me to persuade others that group prayer activates revival in the church and missionary outreach; without it all Christian work limps and falters.[4]

STEPS FOR BUILDING FRONTLINE PRAYER MEETINGS

What steps does the local church leader take to implement this kind of New Testament praying in the congregation? I wish to stress the importance of humility and patience with others when we are captivated by a new vision of what a frontline prayer meeting can do for the body. The leader can easily embrace a new conception of prayer and then outpace the congregation so that he has no one following when changes are introduced. So the first step in teaching about prayer is *to become a better model yourself*, in both private and corporate praying. For instance, have you faced up to the degree your own life and ministry drag because of prayerlessness? If you are the pastor of the church, do you pray for the congregation before you preach—and do you pray afterward for the effects of the Word to continue? Do you pray regularly through the church directory for every member of the church? Do you constantly give thanks before the church for the love of God revealed in the Cross?

To improve your practice of prayer, I can recommend no better helps than Charles H. Spurgeon's "Effective Prayer" and the account of J. O. Fraser's praying in the well-known chapter 11 of Mrs. Howard Taylor's *Behind the Ranges*. Set a simple goal for yourself: not to give yourself and God any rest until you have taken into your own life the lessons on effective praying proposed by Spurgeon and Fraser.

The second step should be *to deepen your knowledge of corporate prayer* by the close study of prayer in Luke and Acts.

---

[4] A major influence on my thinking in this regard has been Jonathan Edwards's essay "An Humble Attempt to Promote Explicit Agreement and Visible Union of God's People, in Extraordinary Prayer, for the Revival of Religion and the Advancement of Christ's Kingdom on Earth," *Works* (Worcester: Isaiah Thomas, Jr., 1808), 3:355–494.

For rich insights into the subject, examine Harvie M. Conn's article "Luke's Theology of Prayer" in *Christianity Today* (December 22, 1972) and David Bryant's excellent book *Concerts of Prayer*. To appreciate the historical impact of corporate prayer, immerse yourself in J. Edwin Orr's book *The Fervent Prayer*, a survey of the effect on the churches of North America and the United Kingdom of prayer for revival by small groups.

The third step is to seize every opportunity *to talk with others* informally about frontline praying. Introduce them to great passages on prayer like Luke 11:1–13 (the friend at midnight) and the pattern of group prayer followed by outreach action found in Acts 1–4. Then when you are with two or three Christians discussing these teachings, suggest that you *pray right then and there* along the lines indicated in Luke–Acts and in this chapter. Whenever you meet anyone with a need, encourage that person to pray with you for the felt need and then to reach beyond to pray for God to send revival to the church and to bring in a missionary harvest.

In his seminars on prayer, David Bryant stresses that every human need ought to be related to the missionary vision of the Scriptures. For example, he says that a Christian may have a felt need to lose weight, but the prayer for strength to diet is not answered because the motivation is self-centered; the person wants to look better for his or her own sake. But let the person change the motivation and ask God for grace to lose weight so as to glorify Him by becoming a more attractive and wholesome witness to Christ; then, Bryant believes, such God-centered praying will prove to be more effective.

The fourth step is, if you are a pastor, *to become more public in your teaching about prayer and in implementing changes* in the programs of the church to give prayer its premier role. Preach a series of sermons on prayer, its nature and role in the normal church. Plan your pastoral prayers more carefully, and pray ahead of time that God will give you grace to speak for the congregation to Him, but doing so deeply aware of His presence rather than the presence of human beings. Arrange for more time to be devoted to prayer at the board meetings of the church.

Do not begin by making radical changes in the format of

the traditional prayer meeting. Start by improving its quality. Reduce your Bible study to twenty minutes, but plan it so that it relates to prayer and the promises of God. In effect you are setting forth the principles of effective praying and have opened up at least fifteen additional minutes for the actual task of praying. Carefully plan beforehand how this time will be used by you and the people gathered for prayer.

Gradually make the changes in the format of the prayer meeting more thoroughgoing. Continually struggle in prayer yourself for wisdom to make the prayer meeting more God-centered and less problem-centered. You are in the toughest battle facing the Christian church. Prayer meetings constantly tend downward, to become either intellectualistic Bible studies or anxiety-sharing sessions where religious arguments break out. Christian people and their leaders are ready to do almost anything except get down to praying with power and authority in the name of Christ.

A WORD OF ENCOURAGEMENT: THE SPY IN THE HEART

By now you may feel overwhelmed by your own inadequacy in prayer. You may also conclude that your congregation does not have any frontline praying at all. But on this point you could make a grave mistake by overlooking the spy who lives in the heart of every believer. I am thinking of the Holy Spirit, who constantly labors in us to open us up to God's Word and will. We may be completely closed off to a line of biblical teaching and not know it, but then in our presumption we end up in situations in the church that threaten to swallow us up. At that time the Spirit begins to force questions upon us, probings from heaven that surface irresistibly in our minds. We may press these down, but the questions persist.

What we are experiencing is the Holy Spirit doing an "inside job" on us, opening doors and letting in truth that seems quite alien to us naturally. And this is always true of prayer. Prayer is always mysterious, partly alien, and to pray effectively is to break through what Richard Lovelace has called "invisible barriers." But released by the Spirit, we do learn to pray as individuals and as congregations. The Spirit is sovereign. Prayer is His gift, and He will succeed in teaching His church to pray.

You may not be the pastor in the local church. But all pacesetters can depend on the spy's living in their fellow Christians to open them up to the approach to prayer set forth in this chapter. You can begin by sharing literature on prayer with your pastor and other officers in the church. As you do, pray for the Spirit to be opening their minds to biblical teaching about corporate prayer and prayer based on the promises of Scripture. You can converse with them as to the meaning and application of the various passages on prayer that are found in Scripture. A leader of the Sunday school can stimulate interest in praying together at leadership meetings and foster the organization of an adult Sunday school class on prayer. You can either lead such a class yourself or select a carefully chosen leader who knows both how to teach on prayer and how to pray.

PRAYING FOR THE PASTOR

Most of all, you can make the pastor sense how much you are behind him by your prayers. I have found nothing more stimulating to my own prayers than knowing that members of the church are earnestly interceding with a heart of love for me and my work in the church and community. One woman in particular at the Chapel in the late sixties was a bridge leading me into the world of prayer. At first I was resistant when she prayed fervently for me and my ministry every Wednesday evening. Gradually this praying began to stimulate my faith, and I began to pray more for my own ministry.

Then, as my heart softened, this dear lady began to ask me questions. She queried me with a smile and without guile, "Since we call it a prayer meeting, wouldn't it be better to have a shorter Bible study on Wednesday evening and give more time to prayer?"

My response was somewhat confused. I asked, "Don't you like the Bible study?"

Her reply won my heart. "I love it, and I really am eager to see more people come to it. But maybe it could be on another night, so that on Wednesdays we could pray more." Gradually I began to devote more time on Wednesday evenings to prayer, and I focused the Wednesday Bible study itself on the promises as a basis for effective corporate prayer. Eventually I began a Bible study on Monday evenings, and as its attendance grew, many of the people who came to Christ because of it began coming to the prayer meeting on Wednesday evening.

I thank God for this faithful Christian woman who was a real pacesetter from God for me and our church. What she did I think most people can do. She prayed for me and the work with power and love. She did it in private, and she did it in my hearing on Wednesday evenings. She also gently entreated me to put the focus in the prayer meeting on praying and then exercised patience with me as I slowly responded.

FULL OF FAITH

Now accept a word of encouragement from the pastor who killed the prayer meeting. At the beginning we do not have to be full of faith. I certainly was not. Nonetheless, as we as leaders travel this path of corporate prayer, we will arrive at a place where we never expected to be, people full of faith, seeing God do mighty things through our prayers and labors. What we have always wanted will come to us as a gift of the King as we pray and as we lead others to pray with us.

It was about 1962 when the prayer meeting died under my inept leadership. More than a decade later when we were considering the beginning of New Life Church, we initiated a small prayer meeting in our home. As we claimed the promise of the Spirit's presence, we found ourselves gripped by the assurance that God was going to work. He did. Two of the people attending the prayer meeting came under conviction and gave their lives to the Lord. From that impetus we decided that it was clear the Holy Spirit was moving and that the King was beginning a harvest in our community.

It's enough to stir your faith to action!

ACTION STEPS

1. List the key elements that lead to the decline or death of a prayer meeting.

2. List the key elements that lead to a prayer meeting's becoming a power source for renewal and missions.
3. Which elements listed under the first two questions are to be found in your local church prayer meeting or meetings?
4. Meet with two other people who attend this prayer meeting, and discuss with them weaknesses and strengths of the prayer time. Share with them several key ideas from this chapter and brainstorm on ways to make the prayer meeting more biblical.
5. Meet again with the two people mentioned above to pray together for your church's regular prayer meeting.
6. Develop a simple plan for improving the prayer meeting. Include the following: Inviting new people to come; focusing a shortened Bible study on the promises; appointing a secretary to keep a record of requests and to report on them weekly; praying ahead of time for each person who is likely to attend; choosing hymns and songs that focus on the resurrection power of Christ.

READING SHELF

BRUCE, A. B. "Lessons in Prayer," *The Training of the Twelve.* London: Hodder and Stoughton, 4th ed., n.d.

BRYANT, DAVID. *Concerts of Prayer.* Downers Grove, Ill.: InterVarsity, 1984.

HALLESBY, O. A. *Prayer.* Trans. by Clarence J. Carlsen. Minneapolis: Augsburg, 1937.

ORR, J. EDWIN. *The Fervent Prayer: The Worldwide Impact of the Great Awakening of 1858.* Chicago: Moody, 1974.

SPURGEON, CHARLES HADDON. *Effective Prayer.* Grand Rapids: Evangelical Press, n.d.

IV

SERVING AS GOD'S MISSIONARY LEADERS

CHAPTER 8

THE PASTOR
AS PACESETTER

We have defined the "pacesetter" as a church leader who wants to have a part in overcoming the introversion of the local church. He or she wants to help marshal its gifts and life for outreach to the world and is able to enlist others to help in this cause.

Our particular purpose is to encourage such a person to do this work *self-consciously* and *intelligently* as guided by the Scriptures and the Holy Spirit. We have sought to indicate where this missionary life begins, how we can recover the missionary identity of the local church, and what the sources of missionary power are for this undertaking. The emphasis has fallen on both the pastor's work and the leadership of the local church in general. This chapter is directed to the pastor in his primary role in restoring the church's outward face. How can the pastor become God's pacesetter in the local congregation? What should he be and do to stimulate an ingrown church to reach beyond its walls into the community and the world beyond?

At first the task would not seem to be difficult. The pastor seems to have everyone's ear and often is greatly respected by members of the congregation. But a little experience in the pastorate reveals that what appears to be simple can prove to be extremely complex. A younger pastor told me recently,

I left a parachurch organization in the inner city to enter the pastorate. My motive was right. I believed that I could reach more people for Christ in the church and through its ministries, so I poured my heart into the work. But now, after several years, I have serious doubts about the effectiveness of a church ministry. Before becoming a pastor, I saw people frequently converted through my efforts. I discipled them and they matured in Christ. But I haven't seen much of that since I became a pastor. It makes me wonder if there is any future in the local church for me.

As we talked, a number of issues came to the surface. It turned out that this young pastor feared that more aggressive evangelism and discipleship would stir up trouble in the church. He was concerned that singling out particular people for intensive training and ministry might stir up jealousy, or at least cause misunderstanding. And he seemed uncertain in his understanding of God's will for the local church. The primacy of the mandate to fulfill the Great Commission had been the foundation of his parachurch ministry, but he was not sure where it fit in the life of the local church.

I do not think this pastor's hesitations were groundless. Any move into the world by an ossified body is bound to cause creaking and groaning in some of its parts. I could also understand his feeling that the Great Commission applies only in the vaguest way to the local body, while his parachurch organization had built its whole life around obedience to the Lord's missionary mandate. As we have seen, the introverted church is characterized by passivity among its members. It is typical of the local fellowship that the Great Commission is seen as having direct reference only to foreign missionaries, evangelists, and pastors.

"And pastors"? There lies the opportunity. The members of a typical church expect us to be full of missionary zeal and usually will give at least nominal encouragement to efforts to reach out into the community.

I began to learn this lesson during my first pastorate. Becoming a pastor turned out to be a great culture shock. Once I had received the title "Reverend," it seemed that I ceased to be a human being for many people, especially for non-Christian friends and neighbors. Before this, my style of witness had been expressed in hospitality and friendships, but when I became a "minister" I learned that the typical neighbor is not ready to rush over to one's house for dinner. For some, such an invitation was like having an evening with a double penalty, akin to a trip to a Billy Graham crusade followed by a visit to death row. You could get both miseries in one evening at the "minister's house."

Of course, not everyone was that sensitive, but once the label "minister" gets tied to you, you are put on a pedestal of religiosity and people are wary of you—and especially cautious about your friendship overtures. One woman told me that it was such a struggle for her to come to our home that she stood immobilized before the doorbell. The only way we met is that I happened to open the door unexpectedly and caught her ready to depart!

But there is, I discovered, a marvelous opportunity here. While I could no longer assume that every neighbor was eager to come over to our home for dinner, other doors opened for me that I never dreamed were there.

I came to see that people who come to church are not at all surprised when a minister asks them questions about their spiritual state. I learned that visitors to church could accept from me a rather direct inquiry about their spiritual life. I began to take advantage of this opportunity as I greeted people at the church door after Sunday morning worship. When a new person thanked me for the message, I would say with a warm smile, "I'm so glad you liked it. Was there anything that especially helped you—any particular thought?" Sometimes I drew a complete blank, with the person not knowing what to say. But more often the visitor would mention an illustration or humorous comment. From there I would gently lead the person to this question: "I appreciate your insight—a good thought. But let me carry it a bit further: Do you see yourself as growing spiritually?"

The question was rarely understood immediately, but it led to further dialogue and to numerous conversions as a result of follow-up.

Emboldened by the responses I was getting from people at the church door, I began to announce from the pulpit that I would stay and talk with anyone who wanted spiritual or personal guidance. As a result of this invitation and open friendliness from the pulpit through the years, scores of people have found Christ after the services. To be sure, this zeal has a cost. For many years I rarely was home from the church building much before two o'clock, and on numerous occasions it was later than that. The price has to be paid, but compared to the reward it is nothing.

In short, people expect us as pastors to be dedicated to God and to have a gracious soul-care for them. Perhaps some will reject our expressions of concern, but they would probably not have responded to Christ anyway. *What I found out is that people come to a church where they are wanted, and they come to the pastor who wants very much to introduce them to Christ.*

INGROWN LEADERSHIP

People commit themselves to a church where they feel wanted. But what do we do as pastors with key people in the church, perhaps even elders or deacons, who do not seem to want new attenders or any element of unpredictability in the established life and order?

Again, the principle applies. Elders and deacons who themselves are ingrown and fearful of change can be led into the harvest field by a zealous pastor. What I have done in such cases is to invite them to go with me in calling on new people. I am amazed at how this visitation can transform the attitude of the elder or deacon. I have found that the brother who visited with me during the week will almost always go out of his way to greet the person the next Sunday.

But what if the stand-pat leader will not go calling with us—or do anything in the way of shepherding God's people? Here we must be tender and patient, but also true to our vision and call. One strategy is to introduce a study of 1 and 2 Timothy for the elders or deacons and let them hear God's standard for them and their work. Afterward try once more to get the recalcitrant leader to join in visitation. If he still declines, we must exercise zeal for this person's spiritual welfare and inquire privately as to the reason for his failure to do the work to which he has been called. After a period of patient discussion, we should ask the nonfunctioning person, "Dear brother, in the light of 1 and 2 Timothy, do you think you have the gifts and calling from God to be an elder (or deacon)?"[1]

It might seem that this question would be an affront to a leader's dignity, but it is much less so if it follows a significant period in which we have drawn close to him and sought to help him fulfill his office. After a period of instruction and loving support followed by his repeated evidence of incompetence, it is usually a relief for the person to resign his office.

But however the person receives our leadership, our duty is clear. As fellow church officers we must humbly accept the correction of others and extend it with all love to them in turn. Introversion among local church leaders exists largely because pastors and elders have neglected their duty to do what Hebrews commands every believer:

> But exhort one another daily, while it is called Today; lest any of you be hardened through the deceitfulness of sin (Heb. 3:13 KJV).

In other words, our exhortation to the nonfunctioning church leader is important not only to the proper government of the congregation but also to the spiritual protection of the elder or deacon himself. There is something deadly about holding an office that we cannot fulfill and then refusing to give it up after loving instruction and admonition. For his own sake the erring person must be confronted by us and the other leaders of the church.

My experience is that it is somewhat rare for correction to go this far. Instead, the real obstacle in dealing with introverted leadership lies more in the fears of the pastor. As I talked with the young leader mentioned earlier, I found that he had the same underlying problem that I had: fear of people and the desire for human approval. We do not wish to rock the boat for fear of suffering ourselves. What's more, we lack genuine love

---

[1] This question should always be based on a study of 1 Timothy 3, which discusses the qualifications of elders and deacons. An excellent study guide for this passage is Gene A. Getz's book, *The Measure of a Man* (Glendale, Calif.: Regal Books, 1974).

for the person who is straying from God's will. I can rationalize my timidity all around the barn and imagine all kinds of terrible scenarios resulting from a confrontation with inert leaders.

CONFLICT-AVOIDERS

But how do we cure this evil—the combined fear of people and lack of love for them? The need of many pastors is to look back to their childhood. Some may discover that as children they loved conflict and thrive on it even today. As adults these people can become pastor-tyrants who abuse church discipline. But most of us who make it into the pastorate are inclined to be like me: a conflict-avoider from an early age. Through the years I have learned to dislike church conflicts and personality clashes with intensity, but I have slowly learned that the kingdom of Christ can only grow through conflicts. In one of his writings Oswald Chambers has said that in discipling, the most difficult pain to bear is that which we must give to others. Causing pain to those we love is, in his view, the greatest cost in discipling. He also makes it clear that such pain is an absolutely necessary ingredient in discipling. If as a pastor-discipler we do not encourage, correct, and exhort, we simply will not see God build His church through us.

More than one pastor has asked me, in light of this, how I overcame my timidity. I feel the force of this question, because I tend to be fearful of confronting authority figures. But I have another fear as well. Back before I became a Christian I had a strong temper that got easily "lost," or shall I say "easily found"? So I am doubly fearful—both of the other person's possible wrath and also of my own.

AN OVERCOMING ZEAL

There is only one thing that has helped me overcome these fears, and it is zeal for the gospel and its effects in the world. When I am living out the gospel—and the gospel is living in me with power—my fears shrink to Lilliputian size. If we walk with Jesus, we will begin to take on both His lamblike gentleness and His lionlike courage.

The gospel must do more than sit on the surface of our minds if it is going to have that kind of control of our character and emotions. We must get it into the depths of our souls until it is the dominant power in our lives. Charles Haddon Spurgeon said this gospel dominance was the sole explanation of his own life and ministry. He said, "Personally, to me, the gospel is something more than a matter of faith; it has so mingled with my being as to be a part of my consciousness, an integral part of my mind, never to be removed from me."[2] In the same lecture he adds vital color to this gospel-conscious life. He says,

> Brothers, I beseech you, keep to the old gospel, and let your souls be filled with it, and then *may you be set on fire with it!* When the wick is saturated, let the flame be applied. "Fire from heaven" is still the necessity of the age. They call it "go," and there is nothing which goes like it; for when the fire once starts upon a vast prairie or forest, all that is dry and withered must disappear before its terrible advance. May God Himself, who is a consuming fire, ever burn in you as in the bush at Horeb! All other things being equal, that man will do most who has most of the divine fire. That subtle, mysterious element called fire— who knoweth what it is? It is a force inconceivably mighty. Perhaps it is the motive force of all forces, for light and heat from the sun are the soul of power. Certainly fire, as it is in God, and comes upon His servants, is power omnipotent. The consecrated flame will, perhaps, consume you, burning up the bodily health with too great ardor of soul, even as a sharp sword wears away the scabbard; but what of that? The zeal of God's house ate up our Master, and it is but a small matter that it should consume His servants.[3]

What Spurgeon would have us see, what he insists upon, is that the pastor be a man whose inner life has been gripped through and through by the message of the Cross. But how did Spurgeon get such a gospel consciousness? As I read his sermons, his lectures to his students, and his two-volume biography, it is clear to me that he deliberately set out to model his own life and ministry after that of George Whitefield, the great evangelist of the eighteenth century. Whitefield had a

---

[2] *An All-Round Ministry* (London: Banner of Truth Trust, 1972), p. 125.
[3] Ibid., p. 126.

double-barreled passion, first for the gospel and secondly for
the souls of men. Though Whitefield was an itinerant evangelist and Spurgeon a settled pastor, the latter caught the
evangelist's vision of faith and passed it on to his congregation.
Zeal begets zeal.

Spurgeon saw in Whitefield and his preaching a complete
giving of self to God. Cornelius Winter, a young assistant
during Whitefield's later years, confessed that "I could hardly
bear such unrestrained use of tears, and the scope he gave to
his feelings." Winter said of Whitefield that "sometimes he
exceedingly wept, stamped loudly and passionately, and was
frequently so overcome, that, for a few seconds, you would
suspect he never could recover, and when he did, nature
required some little time to compose herself."[4]

From this preacher of faith, Spurgeon derived his model
of the man of God in the pulpit and the congregation. His true
preacher was a man who made his life and preaching one great
act of devotion to God, his being a "whole burnt offering," and
his ministry one of such intensity that he risked having "heart
and brain give way."[5]

I do not suggest that the pastor of the local church must
preach with the full evangelical fire of a Whitefield or a
Spurgeon. The point is that in life we often get what we want.
Spurgeon wanted to have something of Whitefield's gospel fire
and he got it.[6] But Spurgeon's central insight is that this zeal is
expensive; it costs your life. His conclusion is that "we can
only produce life in others by the wear and tear of our own
being."[7] But when we give our lives away in this fashion,
when the gospel has burned away our self-centered fears, then
our zeal for Christ will be a purifying influence in the church
and it will inevitably overflow into the world.

The oratorical gifts of both these men were so great that it
would be easy for more typical pastors like me to feel that
Whitefield and Spurgeon are in a world of their own that we

---

[4] Arnold Dallimore, *George Whitefield: The Life and Times of the Great
Evangelist*, Vol. 1 (Westchester, Ill.: Cornerstone Books, 1980), 483.

[5] Spurgeon, *An All-Round Ministry*, p. 177.

[6] For Spurgeon's dependence on Whitefield as a model, see Dallimore,
p. 534.

[7] Spurgeon, *An All-Round Ministry*, p. 177.

cannot approach. Now, I would be foolish to think that I have Whitefield's or Spurgeon's speaking abilities. I am sure my young pastor friend agrees that he does not have them either. We are much better just being ourselves. Yet, as I study the lives of these two men of faith and zeal, I see an element in them that is often missing in me. This crucial element is the way they related to the gospel. They came to it not as strong, sufficient men, as its masters, but as men broken by its teaching about man's sin and God's grace. What the gospel did for them was make them into "weak-strong" men, men weak before God, deeply conscious of their sinfulness, but also strong in the continued, fresh discovery of the pardoning grace of God as revealed in the cross.

While I cannot cite chapter and verse for it in their writings, I know intuitively that the source of their power was their willingness in prayer to be honest before God about their weakness and infirmity. It was out of that honesty that they then experienced His mighty, quickening grace. Faith really moves into our lives when we start telling God the whole truth about our sins, worries, and fears. I think these men were much more honest before God than we modern pastors tend to be.

THE DAY OF LIBERATION

For me the day of liberation came when I began to see that my fears were often rooted in self-centeredness and a desire to protect my own little kingdom. The reason I was immobilized by the self-centered local church was that I myself was self-centered, devoting only a part of me to God. I did not want to put the whole man into the sacrificial fire. But after I gave myself unreservedly to God for the first time in the summer of 1970, I sat down with the elders at the Chapel and began to share with them what I had been learning. I shared my conviction that the church was ingrown and that we needed to repent together for our lack of outward vision.

Afterward almost all the elders thanked me for my zeal for their spiritual welfare and for the church. They even seemed to be pleased by my courage in asking them pointblank about their zeal for Christ's gospel. I was amazed and humbled by such a response to some very plain talk among us.

But in our humanity there is a tendency to lose courage for serving Christ in areas of risk. Our zeal may burn for a while, then burn out. How can it be constantly renewed in us as pastors and in the churches? I believe the answer lies in continuing to do three things:

1. *Meditate daily on the gospel message.* Soak yourself in it. For example, I have tried to memorize all the key passages in the Old and New Testaments that deal with Christ's atonement. Combine that knowledge with frequent meditation on zeal for the gospel as expressed in books like Philippians and 2 Timothy. Then further stiffen your spine by reflecting and praying over the single-minded devotion of Jesus to the will of the Father in the gospel narratives.

2. *Form a prayer group with two other men, where you agree to be honest with one another about your real needs and weaknesses.* Openly acknowledge to these men that you are fearful and self-centered and need grace. Then pray together until you receive it.

3. *Go forward in every part of your ministry.* Act like a courageous person even when you may not feel like one. In anyplace where you feel fear, plunge in. For instance, is there a leader in the church who frustrates you? This is the one to invite to call with you. Is your preaching low-key or downright bland? Resolve from now on to bring every sermon to a climax by preaching the gospel directly to believers and unbelievers, calling them to embrace its saving, healing power.

"Be it unto you according to your faith," said Jesus. So believe, and then go and speak all the words of life.

ACTION STEPS

1. Name an obvious advantage that a leader in a parachurch organization has over a pastor in a local church.
2. Name at least two leadership opportunities that only a pastor can have.
3. Check the areas where you have experienced opportunity blindness:

    _____ Awakening dormant church officers

_____ Recruiting new church officers
_____ Following up people responding to your preaching
_____ Preaching Christ fearlessly and clearly each Sunday
_____ Seeking opportunities to speak in service clubs
_____ Presenting Christ in homes

READING SHELF

BRIDGES, CHARLES. *The Christian Ministry, with an inquiry into the causes of its inefficiency.* London: Banner of Truth Trust, repr. 1967, pp. 239–83.

DALLIMORE, ARNOLD. *George Whitefield: The Life and Times of the Great Evangelist of the 18th Century Revival,* Vol. 1. London: Banner of Truth Trust, 1970.

GETZ, GENE A. *The Measure of a Man.* Glendale, Calif.: Regal Books, 1974.

JEFFERSON, CHARLES. *The Minister as Shepherd.* Manila: Living Books, 1973.

McCABE, JOSEPH E. *The Power of God in a Parish Program.* Philadelphia: Westminster, 1959, pp. 13–30.

SPURGEON, CHARLES HADDON. *An All-Round Ministry.* London: Banner of Truth Trust, repr. 1972.

TILLAPAUGH, FRANK R. *The Church Unleashed: Getting God's People Out Where the Needs Are.* Glendale, Calif.: Regal Books, 1982.

CHAPTER 9

PREACHING BY FAITH:
God's Missionary Fire

The pastoral staff at New Life Presbyterian Church met once to share our individual strengths and weaknesses. After I shared mine, Bill Viss, the evangelism coordinator, said, "Jack, you left out your main strength—didn't even mention it. It's your preaching the gospel all the time—and the way it changes lives."

I had hardly mentioned my preaching, and I was not sure why. Afterward I dug around in the basement of my mind to find some answers. One reason I am reluctant to talk about my preaching is that it is imperfect, and as a person I am imperfect too. So why talk about something that is embarrassing to me because of my lacks?

But there is a deeper reason for my uneasiness in talking about preaching. There is a mysterious element in it. Preaching Christ by faith has an awesome aspect to it: *Christ Himself becomes present and speaks through a feeble human being.* When that happens, something is being put into the preacher and making him into something other than what he is by nature.

This happened to me when I was scheduled to preach to a large congregation near Washington, D.C. During the services I could see some people weeping over their sins. I had not expected this, because affluent Christians today usually do not behave this way. Regardless, a number of people experienced a change in life direction because they took seriously Christ's self-giving on the cross and the issues of heaven and hell.

But the sermon I preached that Sunday was born out of a terrific soul struggle. On my way to Washington on Friday night, I was feeling so low in spirit that there was no way I could preach on Sunday. I was awash with self-pity, so much so that I could not shake it, and I was ready to resign from everything. Yet through a desperate cry of faith, God delivered me.

When I stepped into the pulpit on Sunday, Christ had shattered my pride and freed me to preach Him quietly and simply as the Great Substitute who had kept the demands of God expressed in His law. As I preached, there could be no doubt that He was present, having overcome me, making me what I was not, compelling me to speak tenderly of His unconditional love in Christ.

I first noticed this mysterious, compulsive side of preaching by faith when I was attending Westminster Theological Seminary in 1953. While sitting in John Murray's lectures on systematic theology, I realized that I was really hearing sermons developed with scholarly cogency. Dr. Murray would typically begin a "lecture" in a low voice, perhaps little more than a whisper. You found yourself leaning forward to hear him. Gradually, whenever he treated the subject of Christ's substitutionary atonement, an inner struggle began to take place in him. It was like an invasion from without, capturing the citadel of the man's mind and heart. As a result of this intrusion, his voice would suddenly rise to a shout and then drop to a whisper, only to rise once more with fresh intensity, charged with passion and joy as he spoke of the Lord's self-giving in His atonement.

John Murray could not talk about Christ's death without faith burning in him like a flame. It was mysterious, but from observing this Scot I understood what preaching by faith is all about. It means simply that through the humbling presence of the Holy Spirit in our lives, we have seen the Christ of the Scriptures, and we have fearlessly handed on to our hearers what we have seen.

The permanent effects of this kind of preaching are also mysterious. For if the pastor declares the doctrine of the Cross by faith, he will discover that his preaching has power to dissolve the characteristic features of the ingrown church. Its inward-looking clubbiness, its holier-than-thou defensiveness, and its indifference to welcoming the lost cannot survive the proclamation of Christ's world-embracing love. Members of the congregation will either be awakened to the vision of Christ's global concerns or they will leave the church.

But effective preaching of Christ often issues from painful struggle. In fact, sometimes the deeper the struggle, the greater the joy that comes from it.

On one occasion I was slated to preach at a Bible conference. My sermon was entitled, "Jesus Christ Gentles You." The text was Matthew 11:29: "Learn from me, for I am gentle and humble in heart." After the message something like forty people came streaming forward in tears, without any invitation from me. I spent a brief hour talking with them. Within that span of time, families were reconciled, church leaders were renewed in mutual love after alienation, and I was left astounded by this encounter with God's grace. It was certainly not my doing, for Christ took me by storm.

That is the best way to describe what happened. The event began with intense inward pain, but it ended as a joyous, transforming experience. Christ really is a Tiger, as the poets call Him, and no one can predict when He will leap. That day He dealt with me, the ingrown preacher.

Before I preach I usually look over the congregation and pray that I will be filled with the love of God for the people before me. But that morning, instead of sensing God's love for them, I unexpectedly saw that I did not want to be there at all and did not care a fig for anyone in front of me. Disgusted with myself, I repented wholeheartedly for my self-centeredness.

As I led in prayer before preaching, my mind suddenly filled with God's love for these strangers. Before, I did not want to preach effectively to them for fear they would find their way to my home for counseling, but now my eyes began to overflow with Jesus' love for these people. He took over!

It was all very humbling. Here I was, a seminary teacher and pastor, and my face was wet with tears in the presence of almost four hundred people. You can imagine how puzzled these dear folks must have been.

After the prayer I spoke quietly about the gentleness of Jesus as described in the text. I compared this with the bitterness and burdens of resentment that often clog up our Christian lives without our even knowing it. I pointed the congregation to the Cross as the basis of their forgiveness through faith in Christ. I urged them to come to Christ to find in the Father's love not only forgiveness, but grace to forgive others and to be gentled by this humbling encounter with grace. I assured my now very attentive listeners that Christ would make them gentle.

Christ broke me, and He broke them. We were gentled together. The irony of it all is that none of them apparently needed to come to me for pastoral counseling. They went their way instead with joy. So did I, knowing a bit more about the cost of preaching Christ by faith. It costs the preacher's pride a great deal. For we cannot preach Christ by faith from behind a wall of hubris—at least not with His power and the fire of a living faith.

A UNIQUE GOAL

The experience I have related could prompt one to think that the supernatural element in preaching involves a kind of spiritual magic enabling the preacher to get away with little or no preparation. That conclusion is a grave error. Preaching ought to have the best wit, wisdom, clarity, and logical order that a preacher can give it. But these qualities by themselves will not add up to preaching Christ by faith. Something more is called for.

That something more is aiming the message at people, with the purpose of bringing Christ to them and them to Christ. The goal is to change them by the power of the gospel.

If we as preachers have another goal, we will have short-circuited the whole process and confirmed ourselves and the congregation in our spiritual introversion. I think that we preachers must admit that we often *are* captured by other goals. Sometimes we make an eloquent message our primary goal. We become intent on producing a work of art or a scholarly composition. The sermon can become the end instead of a means toward an end. Phillips Brooks wrote in his

Lectures on Preaching that this is the cause of the failure of so "many of the ineffective sermons that are made." The prevailing intention in the heart of the preacher is to "produce something which shall be a work of art" rather than a message "aimed at the men," with a view to their transformation into Christlikeness.[1]

The preacher can hardly expect the Spirit of Christ to breathe through an art object that exists for its own sake. Often the evidence of a strayed purpose is found in the way the preacher handles the manuscript or notes he uses. He may not be mechanically reading his materials, but you can feel that his real interest is in getting through his composition, not in aiming the truth at his hearers to persuade and move them to embrace Christ.

The preacher should see preaching much more as a declaration of war, a conflict in which well-disciplined words march as to war to bring the hearers to surrender to Jesus Christ. We need to use the pulpit as a battle station.

Surely the ingrown church has been battered and bruised by Satan's attacks. Our powerful ammunition against him and our own flesh is the strong doctrine of the Cross, which is directed to the hearers with winsome authority. Since we are ambassadors of Christ, we have a duty and right to ask our hearers to surrender to Him and His will.

I believe it is easier to say this than to do it. It was one of my students' failures that helped me to see how easy it is to make the purpose of the sermon its own production and delivery. Once while teaching at Westminster, I assigned my students to preach in a nearby church or gospel mission and bring a tape of the message to me for evaluation. One of my abler students handed me his tape, and I took it to my office to listen to it. It was really disappointing. He was not exactly reading the manuscript, but he was heavily dependent on it. I could feel that his interest was not in his listeners, but in the ideas in the manuscript. He droned on in a wooden tone when suddenly loud, booming voices began to break into his message. A true-life adventure was taking place! The recording

---

[1] *Lectures on Preaching* (Grand Rapids: Baker, repr. 1969), p. 109.

equipment in the church was picking up police radio calls. The radio messages revealed that a robber was trapped by the police in a fast-food drive-in restaurant.

Every word the police said had a clear purpose. They meant to capture this man or know the reason why not. I cannot remember a single word from the student's sermon, but I can remember many of the words of the policemen. One of them was yelling to his partners, "Come on! Come on! Over there!"

These men, out there on the street with drawn weapons, knew what they had to do. Their whole enterprise was focused on a single purpose: to capture the man. I think that is our purpose in preaching too: to capture the man for Christ when we preach! Permit nothing in the message that does not serve this master purpose.

WHO CAN DO IT?

I have suggested that preaching by faith is essentially getting a clear view of Christ through the Scriptures and then handing on to others what we have seen. I have further pointed out that this preaching of Christ is often born out of humbling pain. In addition, the message must be aimed in a daring way at the people listening. Obviously this requires moral courage on the part of the preacher. We cannot capture a person without taking risks. But now we must ask, "What kind of person can do this?"

The contemporary clergyman has a highly diffuse concept of his calling if he does not have a core commitment to taking the gospel to the world. He is counselor, worship stage manager, chairman of the church board, peacekeeper between church factions, and organizer of almost everything that must be done well. Today I believe that he also is exposed perhaps as never before to a flow of human miseries and failings. Consequently, he is often filled up to his clerical collar with an awareness, not of God, but of people and the things he must do in serving them.

For such a leader the gospel does not seem to have power to change anyone, including himself. The fires of faith—if they ever burned brightly in his life—have long since been banked, and he does his work, including preaching, in a perpetual state of spiritual exhaustion frequently verging on depression. This can be true in almost any kind of church, but it is especially so in the ingrown, static church where there is no outward success to prop up a weary pastor for the next day's task. For him, depression deepens when he sees all his labor yielding few visible results.

There is a way out, but it is a radical course. It involves taking a second look at our religious busyness and its motivation. We cannot preach Christ by faith unless we have a deep faith in Christ. We cannot cultivate this faith apart from knowing God's awesome holiness, His hatred of sin, and the extent and severity of human sin, including our own. Only as we are gripped by the greatness of our need before God can we understand faith in Christ and experience the spiritual power that faith gives to life. We are not likely to get this kind of faith unless we slow down and take the time to lay hold of the power of the Cross.

Consider the prophetic critique of the contemporary pastor in John Updike's novel *Rabbit, Run*. Jack Eccles, the local Episcopal priest in Mount Judge, is a busybody trying to win the nice-guy award by pursuing Rabbit, the erring Harry Angstrom, who has deserted his wife. Harry is a parishioner of Pastor Kruppenbach of the local Lutheran church.

Kruppenbach says bluntly to Eccles, "You think now that your job is to be an unpaid doctor, to run around and plug up the holes and make everything smooth."[2] The disgusted Kruppenbach adds that Eccles's life is "the story of a minister of God selling his message for a few scraps of gossip and a few games of golf."

To drive home his point, the now angry Lutheran pastor says,

> "You say role. I say you don't know what your role is or you'd be home locked in prayer. *There* is your role: to make yourself an exemplar of faith. *There* is where comfort comes from: faith, not what little finagling a body can do here and there; stirring the bucket. In running back

---

[2] *Rabbit, Run* (New York: Penguin, 1964), p. 137.

and forth you run from your duty given you by God, to
make your faith powerful, so when the call comes you can
go out and say to them, 'Yes, he is dead, but you will see
him again in Heaven. Yes, you suffer, but you must *love*
your pain because it is *Christ's* pain.' When on Sunday
morning then, when we go before their faces, we must
walk up not worn out with misery but full of Christ,
hot"—he clenches his hairy fists—"with Christ, on *fire:*
burn them with the force of our belief. That is why they
come. Why else would they pay us?"[3]

Eccles's real goal in life is to be popular with people.
Since counseling is the way to develop the image of the caring
pastor, he pursues Harry. But he does not bring Christ to him,
or the law of God. He gives him the pop psychology that hangs
like a pink mist over our contemporary culture. Eccles ends up
as a great trivializer, a human being with a weak sense of self-
identity, disguised by his religious activism.

Though in many ways I am not like Eccles, I can see in
myself the same issues of belief and unbelief. I tend to vacillate
between posing as a religious professional who is on top of
things Sunday mornings and at weddings and funerals, and
the obsequious servant who acts as a religious cushion
propping up all the miserable people I meet.

Under the pressure of our times, we feel that every pastor
must be a trained counselor. I agree in part. But I think there is
a terrible danger for us that Updike has pointed out through
Pastor Kruppenbach. It is that we may fail to become men of
faith and instead become human garbage pails collecting all
the "misery" to be found in the ingrown church.

Earlier I said that nothing must go into the sermon that
does not serve its aim to change the hearers. Likewise nothing
must go into the pastor except that which will build his faith
in Christ. When he is a man "hot with Christ," then he is ready
to preach by faith. Nothing less will do. Consequently, we
must repent for our desire to be approved for our everlasting
"stirring of the bucket" of human activity. Preaching requires a
spirit of quietness and waiting on God in prayer. It takes time
to cultivate that style of life.

---

[3] Ibid., p. 138.

FUEL FOR THE FIRE

A crucial element in what I have been saying is the deep-seated conviction that the gospel will renew anyone who receives it by faith. Its message alone has the power to enable the ingrown congregation to outgrow its self-preoccupations. It's virtually a law of preaching: you get what you expect the gospel to do in lives. Assuming you have the gift of preaching, you get results according to your faith, for faith is almost another way of saying *expectation*. Faith within the preacher begets faith within the hearers; unbelief in the preacher spreads its own withering chill and solidifies inward-looking habits among leaders and members of the congregation.

The important point is that the Spirit of grace wants to bring people to Christ, release them from their fears, and fill them with His missionary presence. As preachers we must cooperate with this purpose as we prepare and preach the text, *confident* that Christ will give us His specific application for the particular message, and that the message will transform lives. To put it another way, we must be willing to make fools of ourselves to see this expectation fulfilled.

Matthew Arnold went to hear Spurgeon preach, and then concluded that Spurgeon with his dramatic preaching was something of a fool. But Spurgeon was simply surrendering all his powers to preach the foolishness of the Cross with a confident spirit. Spurgeon was not attempting to preach artistically chiseled messages, but to preach the excellence of Christ, and to do it with all his powers of mind, heart, and body—and to do it by faith. Preaching for Spurgeon was merely aiming the gospel at people's hearts and minds and expecting it to bring them to a knowledge of the forgiveness of sins and the power of a new life. People believed because Spurgeon believed.

Now, how do we as preachers obtain that kind of bedrock, confident faith? We struggle with the message of the gospel until it changes us.

Like Eccles, we pastors are often caught up with wheel-spinning Christian services. But this is not our chief idol. At the head of the idolatrous pantheon is our god of self-exaltation. That is why we can get obsessively overcommitted to our pastoral work. I have in view the many ingrown pastors who work very hard at their shepherding, but for whom the whole ministry is a kind of inward-looking imprisonment. Obviously the introverted pastor cannot overcome the spiritual introversion of the members of the ingrown church.

What lies behind this pastoral inwardness often is a desire to win praise from the congregation. In itself there is nothing wrong with being admired by the congregation. We cannot be effective in a church unless our manner of life commands respect among our hearers. But the love of human applause may involve a desire to be worshiped by our parishioners. Such a stance crowds out the love of God from the heart. It is an issue of consuming awareness, what we surrender to in the inner self. If our minds are almost exclusively on a human valuation of our ministry, then we will have little room for the love of God in our lives and preaching. Jesus once said to His applause-seeking opponents that "you do not have the love of God in you" because they were primarily concerned to receive "praise from one another."

We can often detect this idolatrous love of approval in the way ministers preach. Some come to the congregation Sunday morning like a timid defense attorney presenting a weak case to a hostile jury. Others approach the congregation as though it were an awards committee handing out Oscars for best performance. Either way it is a religious show in which the love of God is displaced by self-consciousness about people and their opinions.

We must admit that we are idolaters, get down on our knees before God like any other fallen sinner, and claim the righteousness of Christ as the sole basis of our forgiveness. Afterward, we can read John 3:16–17 and identify ourselves with the lost world of mankind for which Christ died. We should stay on our knees until we have the assurance that God's love for the "perishing" includes us. Then we can go to the congregation and preach Christ by faith, going as repentant sinners who love God and His people more than we love human approval. If we do this, we will have all the compelling power of God's presence with us.

But the struggle for faith-full preaching does not stop there. A pastor I know is accustomed to preaching through one book of the Bible at a time and commits himself to reading that book at least twenty-five times in English before he preaches the first sermon. I need to read a book of the Bible or a passage of Scripture until it actually controls my thoughts and has begun to change my own life.

I also study intensively the biblical language that relates to Christ's person and work, especially His atonement. I labor with this terminology, using works like *The Apostolic Preaching of the Cross*, by Leon Morris, until I understand the precise meaning of the key texts and can translate their concepts into current idiom. Again, I want my words to march with gracious authority, strong soldiers out to conquer human unbelief. But they can hardly do that if I am smudging over the meaning of passages like John 3:16 with hasty exegesis. I have also memorized large portions of Scripture in English so that the Word of God can dominate my thought life, fuel my faith, and inspire the ardent expression of that faith in preaching.

One last consideration is supremely important. Powerful preaching of Christ cannot be done in one's own strength. For this reason I have recruited several hundred people to pray for me and my preaching each week. This gives me the confidence that God will hear these many prayers offered in my behalf. Sometimes the results of these prayers have been remarkable, bringing to my preaching a depth of sincerity and compassionate concern for people that is not from me.

As a result of this study, meditation, and prayer, I find myself often "hot with Christ" Sunday morning and at other times when I minister the Word of God. What all this fuel does is burn out of me my obnoxious love of being stroked by human praise. I know that I am naturally as addicted to the approval of people as the alcoholic is to his bottle of Old Granddad under the mattress. What emerges for me again and again is an overcoming love of God born of the awareness of His love for me. This love catches fire in my heart and mind when I preach, and sometimes sets my hearers ablaze too.

PREACHING IN A "DYNASTY" CULTURE

I can imagine someone reading all these thoughts and saying, "I have done all this. I have preached Christ faithfully, and nothing much has happened, and I am left in a state of despair about the gospel."

I know how widespread these feelings are among pastors. Of the top twenty preachers I know, as many as half of them are no longer preaching regularly to a congregation. One of them told me recently, "I could not go on. It was too much. In one year *two* of my elders ran off with other women."

It is true that this year's moral failures are worse than last year's. We have "Dallas" and "Dynasty" in our own evangelical backyard. A prominent figure in New Life Church ran off with another man's wife, and we were stunned.

This crisis led me to do some sober thinking about my own preaching and teaching. I concluded that it is easy to think that we are preaching Christ and not really doing so. Edmund P. Clowney, former president of Westminster Theological Seminary, has often said, "A great deal of preaching today is not preaching Christ and grace but mere moralizing."

Too many of us preach messages of duty and responsibility without a foundation of grace through Christ. In other cases, preachers do not show people how to draw by faith on a living Christ and His unlimited resources, but trivialize the gospel message by preaching primarily to *felt* needs. This was Eccles's problem. He tried to help Harry Angstrom with a superficial friendship when Harry really needed a pastor who had been filled with the fire of faith and had the backbone to rebuke him in love for his adultery.

It is not wrong to begin a sermon with an appeal to felt needs. We need to preach where people feel their hurts. But it is wrong not to go beyond these surface issues to *essential* needs. I think we get valuable clues on what these issues are from books like Tom Harris's *I'm O.K., You're O.K.* If Harris is correct, Americans are dripping with guilt, both real and imagined. They are also neurotically defensive in denying their guilt.

To move through this sensitive area to the real need, I believe, preachers must see and make clear to them the character of God as set forth in His law. The Ten Commandments show us our deepest lacks. That lack, in summary, is to love God and our neighbor from the heart at all times. The law says, "Do this, and you will live. Fail to do this and you die."

The law of God thus expresses our inability to be made right and whole by any effort on our part. No human being can stand before a holy Creator who requires perfect love and obedience. Thus all the law can do is to demand unlimited obligation.

Without being taught about the law's demands, people today trivialize the message of the cross. For example, the couple who ran off from our church returned after ten days of earnest prayer by our congregation. But we found that they had trivialized their sin and seemed untouched by any healing fear of God. Unrepentant, both the man and the woman assured us that they still claimed justification by faith as their right, even while holding onto their adulterous relationship.

The congregation responded with love and patience as our elders labored with the erring pair. Finally, the woman came to repentance and gave this testimony,

> I had confused faith and presumption in my mind. What I had thought of as faith was really the presumption that I was a good person who could make it in life without much help from Christ. No wonder I had no strength to resist when temptation came.

She explained that she had known nothing of the severe character of the law of God until one of the women in the church gave her a tape of one of my sermons called "Faith vs. Presumption," a message strongly emphasizing God's right to demand holiness of life from each of us. The repentance of the man followed along similar lines, and today both the man and the woman have been restored to the church and reconciled to their spouses.

It is not the law that transforms the preacher and his hearers. The law awakens us to the fear of God and establishes real needs. But only the gospel can transform and renew lives damaged like this couple's. The law demands perfect love from us, but only the gospel provides Christ, the Great Substitute, who in love kept the law perfectly and paid its penalty on the cross.

Thus the gospel presents Christ as the great object of our faith, and it is His righteousness that is received through faith in His atoning sacrifice (Rom. 3:25). There is no legalism here, no trivializing of grace in the Cross. It is the proclamation of unconditional love manifested in Christ's self-giving that breaks our pride, faces us with God's demand for a holy life, and brings us into the joy and freedom of knowing that the condemnation of the law is *forever* silenced. What a need is then met—to have a conscience freed from divine condemnation!

This freedom ignites people with missionary fire, beginning with preachers. In regard to justification by faith alone, Luther writes,

> . . . Let us conclude that faith alone justifies, and that faith alone fulfilleth the Law. For faith through the merit of Christ obtaineth the Holy Spirit, which Spirit doth make us new hearts, doth exhilarate us, *doth excite and inflame our heart*, that it may do those things willingly which the Law of love commandeth; and so, at last, good works indeed do proceed freely from the faith which worketh so mightily, and which is so lively in our hearts.[4]

When Wesley read this passage of Luther's a couple of centuries later, he said that "he felt his heart strangely warmed." At one stroke he was converted to Christ by the gospel message and made a great preacher. Through his preaching, the world was driven out of many churches and many church members were driven out into the world to witness. Wesley had found God's method for outgrowing the ingrown church.

Our task as pastors is to aim the message at people with courage and command them to believe lest they die in their sins. Our calling is not to put our faith in our excellent sermons but in the excellencies of Christ. Let us, therefore, make our messages sharp-edged instruments to do God's holy work—to inform, to convince, and to motivate, with a view to transforming men and women into the image of Christ through faith in Him alone. Preach Christ with a burning faith, hot enough to get people to listen and catch fire themselves.

---

[4]Cited in A. Skevington Wood, *The Inextinguishable Blaze: Spiritual Renewal and Advance in the Eighteenth Century* (Grand Rapids: Wm. B. Eerdmans, 1960), p. 111.

ACTION STEPS

1. If you are a pastor, review your last three sermons and ask two
   questions:
   a. Did I clearly preach Christ?
   b. Was each message "aimed at men"?
2. Name the deeper flaw underlying Jack Eccles's busyness. Identify
   your own deeper flaws: unbelief? love of human approval?
   ignorance of the gospel and the law? lack of Bible reading and
   study? prayer?
3. Go apart for a day of prayer and fasting. Do the following:
   a. Confess specific failures and sins.
   b. Draw up a weekly schedule that allows at least two hours daily
      for Bible reading and prayer.
   c. Soak in one book of the Bible.
4. Study Martin Luther's *Commentary on Galatians*, especially
   chapters 2–3.

READING SHELF

BROOKS, PHILLIPS. *Lectures on Preaching*. Grand Rapids: Baker,
    repr. 1969.

LLOYD-JONES, D. MARTYN. "The Act of Preaching," *Preaching and
    Preachers*. Grand Rapids: Zondervan, 1971, pp. 81–99.

LUTHER, MARTIN. *Commentary on Galatians*. Grand Rapids: Kregel,
    repr. 1979.

MORRIS, LEON. *Apostolic Preaching of the Cross*. Grand Rapids:
    Eerdmans, 1956.

UPDIKE, JOHN. *Rabbit, Run*. New York: Fawcett Crest, 1983.

V

DISCOVERING GOD'S
MISSIONARY STRATEGIES

CHAPTER 10

EQUIPPING FOR THE HARVEST FIELD

The role of the pastor is unique in its opportunities to break down walls of congregational self-centeredness with the gospel message. Perhaps the most crucial way a pastor can accomplish this is through the task of "equipping," a function Ephesians 4:12 specifically assigns to the pastor-teacher.

The Greek word for "equipping" (*katartizō*) used in this pivotal passage has in it the idea of "preparation" or "equipping for something," according to Arndt and Gingrich.[1] In Luke 6:40 the word is used to mean to "train" or "disciple," when Jesus says, "A student is not above his teacher, but everyone who is fully *trained* will be like his teacher."

This concept of "equipping" suggests that the pastor's primary role is to *prepare* and *train* others for service. The pastor's role today is not usually defined in this way, and this shift in perspective raises questions like these: Will the training of certain members in the congregation by a skilled professional lead to elitism? Will it promote jealousy in those who are not included? Is there a danger that the pastor will work himself out of a job or be replaced by a new co-laborer? And, on a basic level, how exactly do we equip another person?

---

[1] *A Greek-English Lexicon of the New Testament and Other Early Christian Literature* (Chicago: University of Chicago Press, 1957), p. 418.

To answer these questions, let us first examine why pastors often feel uncomfortable with the concept and practice of training others for "the work of service."

I believe a major reason for this pastoral hesitation lies with the established notion of "the clergy" as an elitist class with a unique status that needs to be protected. If we assume that the clergy represent an upper tier of the people of God, standing above the laity, it seems pointless—and possibly wrong—to train laymen to study and teach the Bible when only the ordained minister is really capable of handling the Word.

For many leaders and church members today, there are virtually "two peoples of God," with the *real* people of God being the ordained pastors.[2] Regrettably, this theological error has been reinforced by the King James Version's rendering of Ephesians 4:11–12, the key passage dealing with equipping. It reads:

> And he gave some apostles; and some, prophets; and some evangelists; and some pastors and teachers; for the per-fecting of the saints, for the work of the ministry, for the edifying of the body of Christ. . . .

This translation gives the distinct impression that "pastors and teachers" are to do virtually everything in the church. They are "perfecting the saints," doing "the work of the ministry," and "edifying the body of Christ." Obviously the reader is left with the implication that the essential people of God are the ordained ministers, since the whole service of God is virtually theirs. There is little for "the saints"—that is, the members of the body—to do.

Compare the King James with the Williams translation:

> And He has given some men to be apostles, some to be prophets, some to be evangelists, some to be pastors and teachers, for the immediate equipment of God's people for

---

[2] I do not oppose an ordained "clergy," of course, but rather I insist that there is only "one people of God," not two. The difference between the ordained ministers and church members generally is one of role and function, not of essence. See John R. W. Stott, *One People: Clergy and Laity in God's Church* (London: Falcon Books, 1969), pp. 26–27.

> the work of service, for the ultimate building up of the
> body of Christ . . .[3]

Note that Williams omits the article "the" from before the
word "service," which is his word for "ministry."[4] He also
removes the comma the King James Version had placed after
"the saints" (Williams, "God's people"). In its grammar and
punctuation, the King James breaks the relationship between
the people of God and the work of service of Christ's body,
thereby implying that the ordained ministry is to do practically everything in the church. But Williams's translation
makes clear that the people of God are the primary workers in
building up the body. The pastors-teachers are preparers and
equippers for this work. The pastoral role is an honored but
limited one: to equip the people for *their* work.[5]

BOUND BY TRADITION

We can understand why it is easier for independent Christian
organizations to engage in leadership training. The parachurch
organization and its leaders do not have to struggle against
long years of church tradition that makes the pastor virtually
the sole servant of Christ in the local church. The leader in the
independent agency has the distinct advantage of having his
role defined as that of equipper, trainer, and discipler of others
for the service of Christ. But in the local church, even where it
is not touched by clericalism, the pastor is expected to do the
lion's share of the work. He is often afraid he will be viewed as
a shirker if he does not run himself ragged attempting to do his
work and everyone else's too.

I once visited a church in Florida and enjoyed the church
service, though it seemed that the pastor was a bit harassed.
Afterward a woman in the congregation said in his praise, "He
does so many things in the church. He does all the teaching
and preaching and much of the calling. Not only that, but did

---

[3] Hendriksen, Lenski, Salmond, and Stott all challenge the accuracy of
the Authorized Version's translation of Ephesians 4:12.

[4] There is no definite article in the Greek text.

[5] See William Hendriksen, *Commentary on Ephesians* (Grand Rapids:
Baker, 1967), p. 197.

you see how well he led the choir? And you should see what he and his wife are doing in the Sunday school!"

I suspect that I cowardly mumbled something to her by way of agreement. And I have often been in the same boat— trying to row its many oars while being cheered from shore by approving church members. Let us admit, fellow pastors, that we often find our identity and self-worth being established, or at least shored up, by compulsive work habits. Yet there is in this an insecure egocentricity that leads us to seek acclaim as *the* indispensable servant of God through involvement in every major ministry of the church.

Insecurity in a pastor's life obviously hinders the work and growth of many promising churches. I think of the countless congregations which, inspired by the labors of a single pastor, grow to a membership between 160 and 200 and then stall at that level. Often the hidden cause is that the pastor cannot bring himself to share the burdens with a co-worker or to delegate work to others within the congregation. One example was the pastor of a church this size who called me when I was still teaching at Westminster Seminary. "Can you find a pastoral assistant for me?" he asked. "Just one thing: Please *don't* send anyone who can preach better than I can."

Allied to the fear of being overshadowed is the compulsive busyness in which many pastors trap themselves. Overinvolvement in ministry can alienate a pastor from the gospel and the life of faith it promotes. Gradually and unwittingly caught up in the energetic pursuit of ever-increasing goals, a pastor may begin to feel that he *owns* the work of God, as though he were the head of the church and its sole defender.

David Mains, the former pastor of Circle Church in Chicago, knows how easy it is to fall into this pastoral trap. He laments as he reviews his ministry that ". . . I allowed my own identity to merge with the church."[6] Once our personality merges with the church, it also begins to own us.

If we have enthroned the ministry as an idol, we discover to our dismay that idols have a remarkable power to enslave. As we identify more and more with the work, we find

---

[6]David Mains, "My Greatest Ministry Mistakes," *Leadership* (Spring 1980): 22.

ourselves obsessively concerned to protect it from anyone who might jeopardize it.

A pastor in this position will inevitably find that fear keeps him from his real work of ministry—discipling and training God's people for service. But there is a simple cure for this egocentric insecurity. Notice in Ephesians 4:11–12 who it is who offers gifts to men. It is Christ, the sole Head and Owner of the church. Once that fact is established in our minds, we can renounce our pride and humble ourselves.

Whenever I do this with honesty, I experience an unleashing of the Spirit in my life and ministry through the discovery that I need to do only *one* thing: the will of God. All I need is to obey God's will in its simplicity, and His will for me is to equip others for the work of Christ's ministry.

So the pastor's role is not the head of the church. He is only a member of the people of God, the laity (from the Greek *laos*, "people"). But as a member of the laity he still has a special function as the pastor-teacher preparing the rest for their work in the church and the world. This is no small dignity.

A pastor who understands this concept has the moral and spiritual freedom to approach the practice of equipping with confidence. A full, clear definition of his equipping role can clarify our calling and strengthen our confidence that Christ will empower us to do it successfully.

This conception of our work can be remarkably freeing. To see ourselves as player-coach and not as the whole team frees the conscience from a sense of endless obligation. We abandon the idea that we are the head of the church, the owner of the family of God, and once we let go in this way, we discover that people will follow us much more readily. Though I have never emphasized a clerical-laity distinction, I have in effect tried to disciple the people of Christ from above. But as God's grace infiltrated my life, I grasped something of the essential nature of discipling: find grace from God yourself and then show others how it happened.

The lights clicked on for me in early 1974 when New Life Church was still young. A professional man in our church asked me to have lunch with him. Over our meal he opened up to reveal an ongoing struggle with sexual temptation and his need for help to deal with it. I said, "Look, I'd be happy to pray for you regularly if you will pray for me in the same area." I suggested that we meet weekly for prayer and Bible study. Before long a dozen men were meeting with me to study Luke 12 and its teachings on the personal and spiritual obstacles disciples face. Without my actually planning it, powerful discipling was taking place. Several of these men went on to become elders or deacons at New Life Church.

I was learning that pacesetting for a leader begins with humility, honesty, and a willingness to acknowledge one's own weaknesses. The pastor is to lead as aggressively as a Bill Russell or a Pete Rose—the player-coach struggling, failing, and winning right along with the rest of God's team.

HOW TO EQUIP OTHERS

With that biblical perspective established, we need to know how to equip those whom God has given to us. The work of equipping and discipling consists of two elements in the New Testament: the pastor equips God's people (1) *by teaching them the gospel*, and (2) *by training them to use their spiritual gifts* to serve Christ.

Of these two teaching aspects of equipping, John Stott says in discussing Ephesians 4:11–12, "The chief function of the pastor is teaching, for the chief duty of the shepherd is to feed or pasture his sheep.[7] He notes that the aim of this teaching ministry is not to produce passive listeners, but to "lead them into active ministry."[8] Or, to use the image stressed in this book, to make them pacesetters in Christ's service.

Our preaching of the gospel is what builds people's faith in God and fills them with the assurance of His love, freeing them to witness to the world. The gospel of grace is to be clearly seen as the basis on which all exhortations to duty and pacesetting obedience rest. It is to be taught in the pulpit, in counseling sessions, during prayer meetings, at church planning meetings, in the sick rooms, and in cases of church discipline. As we embrace the message of the Cross in the

[7] Stott, *One People*, p.45.
[8] Ibid., p. 46.

presence of our sins and weaknesses, it becomes to us "the word of faith" living in our hearts and sounding from our lips (Rom. 10:6–10).

The simplicity of this approach may offend the pastor who is looking for a more sophisticated discipling method. He may even wonder if the gospel message has this kind of healing power. Does it really provide the basic power, inspiration, and motivation in discipling? Is its message powerful enough to change people into Christlikeness?

I am absolutely convinced that it will. Consider the typical, introverted church member sitting passively in the pew. What prevents him or her from becoming a pacesetter for outreach? Very likely a heavy-spirited awareness of guilt.

Many men are burdened with guilt about lust. Many women are likely to be oppressed by a general sense of inadequacy arising from failures in relationships. Call it poor self-esteem or what have you, at the visceral level many church members have trouble really believing that their sins are forgiven and that God could love them unconditionally.

When we teach these people that it is their duty to obey the Great Commission, it may seem that we are only adding another legal obligation to their load of guilt, one that they do not have the will to obey. But when the gospel is understood and received, it not only takes away guilt from a troubled conscience, but also gives perfect assurance of the Father's unconditional acceptance of each believer as an adopted child. Through faith, this teaching brings release to the encouraged hearer that empowers him or her to walk in love toward others and to be Christ's witness to the world.

Here lies the glory of pastoral work. We don't have to do many things as far as God is concerned. We are mainly to preach the gospel clearly and consistently. In this way we equip the people of God for their work.

This is the answer to the question, What makes missions and missionaries go? What makes the local church a vital center of missionary enterprise? Constantly hearing of the message of the good news, which overwhelms people with the love of God revealed in Christ, is what does it. This vision of the divine love expressed in John 3:16–17 equips believers to fulfill the missionary imperative stated in Matthew 28:18–20.

It is only as God gives us a John 3:16—consciousness that we can understand the Great Commission as the overflow of God's heart of compassion for the perishing world.

Recall the expression "all the nations" in Matthew 28:19. We saw in chapter 4 that it not only refers to the world's people groups, but also to the goyim, "the outsiders," "the enemy," "the God-haters," and "the unwashed." The message of John 3:16 is that these alien folds are all the subjects of God's love. The Creator loves the world in all its nastiness and tells us to proclaim to it the message of His mercy.

It is helpful to me personally as a pastor to recognize this truth. God loves me in all my unworthiness as one who was once among His enemies. By the grace of God alone I stand under this love and impart a message to the local church, a message that breaks down my introversion and that of each believing church member.

But a question arises here. Why is it that many evangelical pastors preach the gospel without seeing this kind of fruit? I believe this happens because the gospel is either being trivialized by being separated from God's law and majesty, or it is not being applied concretely to the needs, fears, and values of the congregation. And that is where the pastor's role as a trainer enters in. The pastor must teach his people to face specific sins and fears, to apply the spiritual power of the gospel to put them to death, and to use the resulting freedom to exercise gifts in service to Christ.

As believers learn to face and forsake specific kinds of disobedience and see the power and love of God applied to their lives, a desire to serve God effectively will grow within them. When the felt need for training arises, it is usually fairly easy to set up either of two kinds of programs: one for training church officers and one for preparing Christian workers.

These programs need to highlight God's love and the life of faith flowing out of that love. They should not simply teach people to manage the machinery of congregational life. A good way to achieve the right goals is for church officers to study Galatians, with its emphasis on the grace of God, followed by a study of 1 and 2 Timothy. For the training of Christian workers, we might follow the outline set forth in John Stott's *Our Guilty Silence*. This is balanced between six weeks of doctrine and six weeks of evangelism training.

Along with others at New Life Church, I have helped develop a leadership training program that is made available to our members under the guidance of the World Harvest Mission training staff. This program and its training manual grew out of experiences in discipling and mobilizing over a period of a dozen years. It focuses on these qualities:

1. Understanding justification by faith and our adoption, and using this assurance of God's love to develop—
2. Regular early morning devotions,
3. Tongue control,
4. Skills in journal-keeping, discipling, and witnessing,
5. Gift identification,
6. Capacity to work within a team and small groups

This program is the most formal and intensive one we offer at New Life, but discipling continues to exist in many other forms there, including mini-churches, Bible studies, and one-on-one relationships.

EVALUATING THE EFFECTIVENESS OF DISCIPLESHIP

Whatever training method we use, the question we must ultimately ask as disciplers is how to evaluate whether we have effectively equipped our people for service. What will we see in their lives that was not there before? I submit that a willingness to reach out with the gospel to the "unwashed" is the mark of a transformed heart and life. A disciple with that commitment has experienced God's love in Christ and aligned his life to Christ's missionary mandate so that others may share it. That commitment is life-changing and plain to see.

When God began a new work in my life in 1973, my sense of God's pardon and acceptance was so deep that His love *for* me became a love *in* me for others. In August of that year I started visiting a local fast food drive-in to talk with the wildest set of teenagers I ever met. After three months of weekly visits, one of the wildest of the bunch found the same love of Christ that I had found. Empowered by the gospel, Bob Heppe gave up his dependence on alcohol and drugs, graduated from high school, went to Temple University, graduated with high honors, and became an evangelist in our church.

In 1981 he went to Uganda as a missionary, but before he left, he led another young man to Christ named John Songster. Bob had initially discipled John and asked me to finish the work so that John could join him in Uganda. I was willing, but I wasn't sure how it should be done. What method should I use with someone so unlike me in background and experience?

The first thing I did was to decide whether John was "disciplable." This is a crucial step in any discipling process, for we cannot effectively disciple anyone who is actually a counseling case or a discipline problem.[9] I gave John a variety of assignments just to see if he was an obedient person. He proved to be a willing worker and quite ready to serve the poor by doing things like painting a room for a person who could not afford it.

After he had completed this series of assignments, I met with John weekly for an hour to disciple him in the Scriptures and the practice of prayer. For the first three months we concentrated on just two general issues: (1) understanding the gospel through the study of Galatians with its relevance for tongue control and forgiveness, and (2) establishing a consistent devotional life.

Next I had John pass on what he was learning to another person. We began to meet weekly with Angelo Juliani, another recent convert who had been local bartender, drug dealer, and big-time operator in the community. During these meetings John handed on what he was learning about "justification by faith" and his new discovery that "sanctification is also by faith." Often as we sat eating our "Big Macs," I would be deeply moved to see how effectively John was discipling Angelo and how both were growing in the knowledge of God.

Soon afterward, John went to Kampala, Uganda, to develop small painting companies, a self-help project for Ugandan believers. He discipled about ten Ugandans in the Bible and in the skills of running a small company, so successfully that at the end of only two years he was able to hand it over entirely to the Ugandans to run by themselves.

---

[9]Counseling is in part a form of discipling, but if the person is immobilized by unbelief or rebellion, our task is really preparatory to discipling.

Angelo became the youth director at New Life Church and has discipled a large number of adults and young people since that time of training in 1982.

There exists today a web of discipling relationships that has spread in all directions and overseas. Moreover, Bob Heppe and Angelo Juliani are now both sons-in-law to me. Angelo said to me once, "Dad, you should have seen the look on your face when you first met me!" It was not exactly a look of approval. But if we preach the gospel with love and let it control our relationships with others, we can watch the change that takes place in us repeated in those we disciple. I know it's true, for I was there.

ACTION STEPS

1. Explain in your own words the statement: "Once your personality merges with the church, it also begins to own you."
2. List ways the church "owns" you.
3. According to this chapter, what is the simple key to release from this bondage? Write your answer.
4. Define: a. Equipper
   b. One people
   c. The relationship between God's love and the Great Commission
5. Outline a simple program you can use for discipling and training church officers.

READING SHELF

KRAEMER, HENDRIK. *A Theology of the Laity*. London: Lutterworth, 1958.

MAINS, DAVID. "My Greatest Ministry Mistakes," *Leadership* 1, no. 2 (Spring 1980): 15–22.

STOTT, JOHN R. W. *One People: Clergy and Laity in God's Church*. London: Falcon Books, 1969.

———. *Our Guilty Silence*. Downers Grove, Ill.: InterVarsity, 1969.

VI

DEVELOPING GOD'S MISSIONARY PROGRAMS

CHAPTER 11

OPENING A WINDOW
OF OPPORTUNITY:
Diaconal Witness

In his book *How Churches Grow*, Donald McGavran says that congregations flourish when "radiant personal faith" is combined with natural "bridges" like family and friendship connections.[1] And he is right.

McGavran is commenting primarily on the personal and family connections of individual believers. But as pastors and leaders in the local church we also need to see that the congregation as a whole can be mobilized to use natural bridges to win others to Christ. The work of the deacons in particular has enormous potential as a means for building bridges between the church and the world.

One community was opened up to witness through a single diaconal act in a local church. The church was Christian Reformed, with a strong Dutch ethnic flavor. Very few people apart from the Dutch in the local community came to the church services. Barriers were high on both sides. But then came a storm that blew the roof off the home of a widow in the neighborhood. She had no means to make the necessary repairs. Spotting the problem, the deacons of the congregation got together, quickly raised the money to pay for the materials, marched over, and replaced the roof with their own hands.

---

[1] Donald McGavran, *How Churches Grow: New Frontiers of Mission* (New York: Friendship, 1966), p. 56.

The attitude of the entire community toward the church changed directions by 180 degrees. Distance and suspicion were replaced by respect and even admiration. For the first time, evangelism in the community began to bear fruit.

Opportunities like this one continually present themselves to members of the local church, but too often we do not have the eyes to see them. One cause of our *opportunity blindness* is our proper theological concern that we not forget the gospel as "liberal do-gooders" in the pursuit of social action. There *is* a genuine danger here. We can lose the gospel and our personal sanity in the swamp of human needs found all around us.

But the church must still have a corporate witness to her neighbors. It is our deeds of love that show forth the glory of the God who called us out of darkness into His marvelous light. And the deacons of the local church can become the pacesetters for a congregational witness by word and works.

This point of view is not new. In the eighteenth century Cotton Mather urged Christians to band together to do good in the neighborhood of their local churches. In *Bonifacius, An Essay Upon the Good*, Mather asserted that the formation of small groups would be a compelling demonstration of Evangelical faith, and that people would be won to Christ when their hearts were softened by deeds of love.

CHRIST THE GREAT DEACON

Mather's basic idea was to see clusters of believers who "would now and then spend half an hour together by themselves, in considering on that question, WHAT GOOD IS THERE TO BE DONE?"[2] His goal was that *every* believer be encouraged to develop an eye for human need, to see "who is in any special adversity; and what shall be done to help them."[3]

Was Mather a liberal activist? Far from it. He was simply drawing out the implications of the gospel and God's love for the world, the master concept behind all our harvesting efforts.

---

[2] *Bonifacius, An Essay Upon the Good* (Cambridge: Harvard University Press, Belknap, 1966), pp. 65–66.

[3] Ibid., p. 66.

Diaconal ministry should spring from our understanding that Christ redeemed us by a servant-deed of love in His atonement. In our caring we follow His example.

Romans 15:8 describes Jesus as "a deacon" or "servant of the Jews" in order that by His death He might purchase the gentiles for His kingdom. Other Greek words used to describe the servant role mean serving as a slave, serving for wages, or serving as an executive under a higher leader. But the word used by Paul in Romans 15 means "a service of love."

According to Hermann W. Beyer, this word, *diakonos*, "has the special quality of indicating very personally the service rendered to another."[4] And it is this word, with all its overtones of intimate love, that is used by Paul to describe Jesus. He is the great Deacon, humbling Himself to the utmost in love for the sake of our redemption. This same word is used elsewhere in the New Testament to describe the work and ministry of deacons in the churches.

Thus the title "deacon" has overtones of deep caring. "Others before myself." In His self-sacrifice Jesus served us by dying for us. The powerful echoes of that work are caught up and sounded abroad in the gospel. It would be strange, then, if the message of the Cross was ever to be dissociated from loving deeds that demonstrate this love to a dying world. Deacons must be seen as the "shock troops" of love. Like Stephen and Philip, they are filled with the Spirit to venture forth for God, doing deeds of kindness and preaching the gospel with courage.

But can this demonstration of love be carried forward by the local church? To accomplish this we must bring together two things: the gifts and resources of the congregation and the needs of the local community. Any outreach coordinated with diaconal ministry requires both kinds of information. If there is an active team of deacons in the local church, the deacons themselves can survey the congregation for spiritual gifts and survey the neighborhood for human needs.

But a word of caution is in order for anyone who undertakes a gift survey in a stagnated church. Some folks may

---

[4] *The Theological Dictionary of the New Testament*, ed. Gerhard Kittel (Grand Rapids: Wm. B. Eerdmans, 1964), 2:81ff.

find it threatening. As you seek to identify skills to be used for service in the community, those who like the status quo may require extra pastoring. Be a good listener, don't force your own will, and continually set forth the biblical basis of this diaconal ministry. But persevere in the survey, and over a period of time the work will be accepted as part of a *new* status quo by the more conservative members.

When it comes to seeing needs in the community, we may find that there are good reasons why these needs have not been noted before. A chief reason is that people with diaconal needs—the sick, the dying, the poor, and the despairing—are usually not attractive, and sometimes they have fallen into their problems through their own efforts. It is easy for deacons to start looking for the noble, deserving poor and to discover that such people are in very short supply.

But we forget good doctrine when we think this way, specifically, the biblical teaching on mankind's fall into sin. Contrary to some contemporary theologians, there is a healing power in the doctrine of original sin. When we go out to serve others, we will often find ourselves taken advantage of. It's unavoidable. Yet when we remember what a great pit *we* were pulled from by the Head of the Church, and what it cost the King in His self-sacrifice, we will be rebuked, humbled, and given persistence to pull others from the same pit of human depravity.

Through the years, my wife Rose Marie and I have used our home for diaconal ministry to people who in many cases had no other place to go. We have taken in people from state mental institutions, troubled children from various agencies, and young people from the drug culture and occult involvement. Our ministry during the seventies was gradually taken over by Dan and Betty Herron, who pioneered the same kind of outreach through the establishment of a diaconal ministry, a home for needy people called Hillside House.

Through the struggles with strangers in our own home and those of Hillside House, we learned a great deal about human corruption. Along with the Herrons, we learned to endure as a daily sacrifice the depressions, the laziness, the ingratitude, and sometimes the slander of those we welcomed into our lives. But in the conflict I found that I grew as a pastor in an amazing way, partly because my own heart was often revealed in all its ugliness and insincerity.

I found it especially hard to be slandered by those who had found a warm welcome in our home. I cannot think of a more crushing experience than to rescue a person from suicide or deep depression and then have that person tell mutual friends that you and your wife are thoughtless, uncaring people—and to have the friends believe the false report and leave the church without an explanation! Events like this have happened more than once.

But the blessing in all this is that we learned that we cannot really love God unless we hate evil—and we need to hate the subtle evil in ourselves as well as the blatant evil we meet in others. I also learned that kingdom power works by forgiveness. What gives vital strength to a ministry to the weak and rejected is a willingness to be weak and rejected ourselves—to confront sin in others with love, and to keep right on forgiving when we are wronged. When that happens in our lives we have at last become the pastors of souls.

EXPERIENCE THE BEST TEACHER

The best training I ever received for pastoral ministry was this diaconal experience, wrought out in travail. An incident that happened in 1974 illustrates this truth.

A young woman who had been deeply involved with the occult, drugs, and motorcycle gangs was living with us. As the gospel began to touch her life, the dark powers at work in her heart stirred her up to plan to murder my wife and me. One day in a spasm of guilt she blurted out, "I've been planning to kill you and Mrs. Miller!"

I was stunned—completely appalled by the depths of evil now being exposed. This young woman who had been soaking up our care, hospitality, and friendship, was intent on committing murder.

Almost immediately I knew what the Lord would do if He were there. I said to her, "Gwen, before anything else happens, I want you to know I forgive you. I forgive you for planning to murder us."

Now it was Gwen's turn to be stunned. She fell back as

though I had struck her across the face. She cried out, "You are the only people who have ever loved me, and I have been wanting to kill you! I am so sick!"

"It shows," I said, "that you cannot change yourself and that I can't either. Gwen, you need Jesus in your heart. Let's pray!"

Gwen made a profession of faith in Christ, and her life seemed to undergo a marked change for the better. I know I was growing like never before, and it made me realize that pastors who shun diaconal ministry cut themselves off from the privilege of suffering for Christ and experiencing the immediacy of His resurrection life.

Diaconal ministry like this confronts an ingrown congregation with the fact that there can be no power of the kingdom working in church leaders and members who are, in their own minds, superior to others—the "sinless" types who identify more with the Pharisees than with Jesus, the friend of publicans, prostitutes, and sinners. Such people have no need for forgiveness and have no intention of extending it to others.

This is the supreme cause of *diaconal blindness* in the local church. We have forgotten how great our own sins are, and feel, perhaps unconsciously, superior to the "unwashed" sinners around us. We would rather be their judges than their servants or deacons. The irony is that we commit our worst sin when we judge others in this way, assuming without warrant that we have no real sins of our own and that we are worthy to sit in judgment on them.[5]

ORGANIZING FOR MINISTRY

Our most important task in organizing and preparing for a diaconal ministry is to tame our own proud hearts. But I am not suggesting a maze of tortuous self-examination. We will get all the humbling we need as we sit by the bedside of the dying, carry hot meals to the sick, visit the nursing home's forgotten people, and welcome poor people into our homes. The idea is

---

[5] For exposure of this trap see especially Romans 2:1 and James 4:11–12. Both passages give severe warnings about judging and despising others out of self-righteousness.

to repent as we go, humbling ourselves as we figuratively wash the feet of others.

Moving a diaconal ministry forward requires careful planning, especially in the development of job descriptions for particular deacons. The needs we will encounter call for different gifts, and no deacon can be assumed to be blessed with every one.

In general, it appears to me that diaconal gifts divide along the following lines and that most deacons fit well into one of these:

1. Exhortation (building faith, encouraging, and correcting)
2. Giving (hospitality, and sharing material things)
3. Administration (ruling as a servant executive to a leader)
4. Mercy (kindness to the sick and sorrowing)
5. Helps (serving leaders, direct caring for the poor)[6]

A deacon may have more than one of these gifts, but the most important quality for a deacon is to be a person strong in faith, willing to serve others, to see "who is in any special adversity; and what shall be done to help them." But this biblical list shows the nature and function of different diaconal gifts. A deacon with the gift of administration may spend most of his or her time organizing work rather than laboring directly with people in need. A believer with this gift must guard against losing touch with people and with Christ's servant heart, but nonetheless not feel guilty about majoring in organizational work.

How should this work of the deacons be structured? In many churches there is a standing board of deacons. But at New Life we had some painful experiences following this model. When our elders created a board of deacons, we unwittingly established a second center of authority for decision making in our church. The effect was to bind up the work of the deacons in the decision making that really belonged to the elders, and to create tensions with the elders whenever they came to different conclusions from the deacons on crucial matters. Happily, God gave the deacons grace to

---

[6]Cf. C. Peter Wagner, *Your Spiritual Gifts Help Your Church Grow* (Ventura, Calif.: Regal Books, 1979), pp. 59–60.

suggest that we dissolve the "board of deacons" and adopt a more flexible organizational style.

Since that time we have developed three classes of deacons at New Life Church: deacons who work on special ministries like nursing home outreach, those who serve through the framework of our church's small-group structure (mini-churches or house churches), and general deacons who serve the congregation at large by collecting funds for diaconal work and making decisions with the elders on its distribution. In each instance the deacons are expected to serve under the leadership of an elder or several elders.

For churches not having a small-group structure, I recommend two kinds of deacons: general deacons who care for the needs of the whole body, and ministry deacons who concentrate on particular areas of service and outreach in at least these crucial areas:

—Hot meals for the sick and for families with new babies (most effectively organized by women deacons in most cases);
—Hospital visitation in coordination with the pastor, including sending flowers to the patient;
—Visitation and evangelism in nursing homes;
—Hospitality and ministry to groups with special needs, such as foreign students, refugees, and single parents.

In all this, the pastor's role is to train and prepare the deacons for their labor of love and to help them structure their work.[7] We can train the deacons to see human needs by taking them with us on hospital and nursing home visits, by alerting them to the practical needs of those who are sick in the church or community, by training them—and the rest of the congregation—to make such needs known to church leaders when they arise. We might help them begin a hospitality ministry by reading a book like Karen Mains's Open Heart, Open Home with them, and developing strategies to apply its principles to our congregations. Perhaps the deacons will choose a home to

---

[7]For guidance in training deacons, see John Guetter, That They May Serve (Grand Rapids: CRWRC, 1981), and Timothy Keller, "Resources for Deacons" (Decatur, Ga.: PCA, 1985).

serve as a model for hospitality, to guide others to do the same things in their own homes.

But there is something further: the praise of God, which must always be the center of this kind of work. Deacons must always be chosen because they have an eye of faith, the capacity to see and publicize the glory of God. This was the strength of Stephen, one of the first deacons chosen in the early church. He was a man "full of faith" who centered all his work on honoring God. He had an eye trained to see windows of diaconal opportunity in the care of the Jerusalem widows and the doing of "wonders" of mercy. But he also self-consciously focused all attention on "the God of glory" as the hidden author of these deeds of love.

How can deacons function like Stephen today? Most churches do not have provision for them to speak and teach as Stephen and Philip did in Acts 6 and 7. This is where the pastor can help. With the concurrence of the church officers, there should be regular opportunities, perhaps monthly, for deacons to report on their work in the worship services and give God the praise for whatever good things have taken place. Glorifying God means to give Him the *publicity* for what He has done in and through His people.

It is true that some aspects of deacons' work is private. For instance, we can hardly stand up and announce that three hundred dollars was given to help a single parent pay the rent. Almost instinctively we sense that such a disclosure is inappropriate. But suppose that after a woman's major surgery, hot meals were supplied to her family through the deacons. It is likely that after her recovery, she or her husband would want to praise God publicly for the healing and the church's care. In some instances, shy believers might write a letter of thanks that a deacon could read, always being careful to honor God for the grace to demonstrate His glory.

Naturally there is the danger that the church will begin to glory in its own power to minister and forget about Christ's supplying the spirit for doing these good works. But if the leaders of the church watch and pray, they can rely on the Spirit and the Word to guard their hearts from falling into a wrong-headed praise of their own goodness.

So stir your faith to action.

ACTION STEPS

1. Write a brief definition of "opportunity blindness." Name the "supreme cause" of diaconal blindness.
2. State in one sentence Cotton Mather's method for overcoming "opportunity blindness."
3. List four things you can do now as a pastor to train the deacons for outreach.
4. At a deacons meeting spend one hour brainstorming on identifying areas of opportunity for "doing good" in your community. In preparation have each deacon read Frank Tillapaugh's book *The Church Unleashed*, which tells how a downtown church can minister holistically to opportunity groups in the city.
5. Choose one target group for your deacons to work with. The pastor should help to develop the program and implement it.
6. Arrange for monthly reporting in the Sunday services on the deacons' work.

READING SHELF

CONN, HARVIE. *Doing Justice and Preaching Grace*. Grand Rapids: Zondervan, 1982.

DE JONG, P. Y. *The Ministry of Mercy for Today*. Grand Rapids: Baker, 1952.

FLETCHER, WILLIAM. *The Second Greatest Commandment*. Colorado Springs: NavPress, 1983.

GUETTER, JOHN. *That They May Serve*. Grand Rapids: Christian Reformed World Relief Committee, 1981.

KELLER, TIMOTHY. "Resources for Deacons." Decatur, Ga.: Presbyterian Church in America, 1985.

MATHER, COTTON. *Bonifacius, An Essay Upon the Good*. Cambridge, Mass.: Harvard University Press, Belknap, 1966.

WILLIAMS, JUNE. *Strategy of Service*. Grand Rapids: Zondervan, 1984.

CHAPTER 12

SMALL GROUPS
FOR OUTREACH

In this book we have looked at the ingrown church and its characteristic failings. We have found behind its many weaknesses a premier failing: our shared unbelief as leaders and members of congregations. To help the leader-pacesetter reestablish the ascendancy of faith in his own life and in that of the church, I have sought to lay a basis for renewal through study of the missionary mandate of our Lord, stressing the priority of the promise of the Spirit as the enabling power of Christ for fulfilling His missionary purpose in the world. In this context of faith, I have shown that the nature of the church is to belong to God and not to itself, and its missionary purpose in the world is to take the gospel to the nations.

We have further learned that the church expresses its missionary identity through deeds of love, motivated by concern for God's glory and empowered by constant corporate prayer. I also stressed that the natural way for a "commissioned church" to express its identity is through hospitality. It is to see itself as a welcoming fellowship. The pastor becomes Christ's pacesetter, modeling and teaching this open outreach style. Above all, he is a gospel preacher, building his own faith and that of the congregation by a burning zeal for proclaiming God's unconditional love for sinners.

But now we face a major problem. What are the most effective ways for implementing this welcoming vision? One answer lies in the previous chapter: the work of the deacons. Another is the ministry of small groups, the subject of this chapter.

By small groups I mean gatherings of believers that can vary in size from about six to thirty. It is my view that such groups today can become the powerful instruments of the Spirit for both internal revival in the local church and its missionary expansion.

HIDDEN POTHOLES

At the same time I have found that this particular road to the missionary growth of the local church has its hidden potholes, and I have pastoral bruises to prove it. For instance, in the work of Hillside House and our home, we discovered that small-group ministry can be exhausting in its demands if it is centered exclusively on the egocentric needs of troubled persons. Some who came for help were gentle lambs needing only nudges to find their way to the green pastures, but others were more like the people described in Daniel Yankelovich's *New Rules,* confused folks with a "rage for self-fulfillment" misled by "an entire literature of pop psychology" fostering in them a "me-first strategy."[1]

Furthermore, our experience with small groups at New Life Church suggests it is easy for them to become protective spiritual nests for garden-variety people. These groups do a wonderful job of assimilating new people into the congregation. But they can quickly develop what Frank R. Tillapaugh has called "a rear-echelon ministry" outlook. The members of the group can meet, talk, and plan almost endlessly, without much happening, with the result that they tend to end up complaining and becoming critical of one another. The reason? They lack clear outreach goals and methods for fulfilling them. The leaders and members are without, in Tillapaugh's words,

---

[1] *New Rules: Searching for Self-Fulfillment in a World Turned Upside Down* (New York: Random House, 1981), pp. 234–37.

"front-line" vision, having only a maintenance-style orientation.[2]

Here is what I have seen happen more than once in small groups at New Life Church, both in the cell-group size of about six people and in the larger size of twenty-to-thirty people. Over a period of time the members of the group become close friends—an excellent development in itself—but drop their non-Christian friends and fail to make any new ones—an unmitigated disaster from the standpoint of the Lord's missionary will. When this trend takes over, faith is stifled and a sense of group superiority begins to prevail among the "disciples." Fear of the world "out there" begins to grow in hearts. Such a stagnating group is quickly and totally demoralized when one of its withering members returns to the "me-first strategy" of our time and falls into sin such as adultery or alcohol abuse or drug addiction.

Having given this warning, I fully endorse the ministry of small groups and would not be without them in any church I would serve as a pastor. I see what Christ has done in our Hillside House, through our own home, and the variety of small groups in our church. In my mind's eye I see the many people who have been transformed in life and character through these ministries.

I also believe that small groups can become the vehicle for harvesting unbelievers in our time. Self-realization as a goal of life is not working well in our time, especially in regard to the family. Yankelovich points out that this "rage for self-fulfillment" is very widespread, with many Americans being involved in a crazy attempt to "realize" themselves—with this unhealthy egocentricity leading to the massive breakdown of family life.[3] Frustrated in this crucial part of human existence, many Americans are, according to Yankelovich, ripe for a new "ethic of commitment" and could be drawn into a "quest for the sacred."[4] His insight is confirmed and powerfully dramatized in movies like *The Big Chill* and *Places in the Heart*—films that speak to a troubled vision in the minds of Americans

---

[2] *Unleashing the Church: Getting People Out of the Fortress and Into Ministry* (Ventura, Calif.: Regal, 1982), pp. 122–23.

[3] Yankelovich, *New Rules*, pp. 234–37.

[4] Ibid., p. 243.

and suggesting that many people yearn for identity in community and to experience forgiveness.

However, I am totally convinced that groups without commitment cannot rise to meet the opportunity that is presented by the frustrations of our time. Gentle discipling is always in order, but "soft discipling" will not do the job in the runaway world of the late twentieth century.

So it is crucial for leaders like pastors to have a clear concept of what these groups should be and do and of the role of the members. It is my conviction that they become effective only if each group member is viewed as a *worker* for Christ, not a mere survivor. The groups themselves should be seen as *growth groups*, a point of view effectively advocated by Win Arn and Lyman Coleman. By "growth groups" I mean that they are gatherings of workers committed to reaching the lost through mutually strengthening faith, assimilating new members, and subdividing upon reaching a certain size.

When I as a pastor consider a new concept for ministry, I usually have a few nagging questions in the back of my mind. You may have the same in your mind. For instance, it is natural to ask, What are the biblical roots for this concept of the small group in the church? Will it work in our time? Has it been tried with good results in times like these in church history?

It seems to me that the biblical roots of the small groups are to be found in the household gatherings described in the Book of Acts. After the events of Pentecost described in Acts 2 we see a combination of large-group worship at the temple with small-group meetings taking place in homes. Through these small groups, non-Christians were daily being added to Christ and the fellowship of the newborn church. Moreover, it seems that Jesus' instruction of His disciples was something like the ministry of a small group, a pattern of working that has been fully described in A. B. Bruce's *The Training of the Twelve* and summarized in Robert Coleman's *The Master Plan of Evangelism.*

As to the effectiveness of small groups in times somewhat like our own, we have only to examine their role in the eighteenth century to discern their power as missionary and revival vehicles.[5] This was a century dominated by materialism, rationalism, and sensualism. The poorer people of England were as a whole degraded almost beyond belief. Drunkenness was so rampant in families that sessions of the English parliament were given over to discussing the problem and seeking an answer. Christianity was typically viewed as a stale joke, its intellectual standing so low that Bishop Joseph Butler wrote, "It is come . . . to be taken for granted by many persons that Christianity is not so much a subject for inquiry; but that it is now, at length, discovered to be fictitious."[6] Many clergymen openly acknowledged that they were not converted, and some vigorously defended the notion that conversion was not necessary for admission to the ordained office.

In this hostile setting small groups were developed as fellowship societies for preserving faith, enabling Christians to survive. But under the inspiration of George Whitefield and the Moravians, small groups were also organized with a missionary direction. The basic idea of the latter groups was not survivorship but *warriorship*. One observer said of the crusading spirit of these groups, "The members of the Moravian Brethren consider themselves storm troops, warriors who at the first call were to be summoned."[7]

But it is Wesley's concept of the small group that has instructed my own thinking and sharpened my practice in their development. Wesley was basically dead-set against the idea that *any* Christian had a right to think of himself or herself as a passive observer, a nonworker in the harvest.[8] He took multitudes of people who were poorly paid, poorly housed, and poorly fed—people who worked twelve hours a day six

---

[5] See A. Skevington Wood, *The Inextinguishable Blaze: Spiritual Renewal and Advance in the Eighteenth Century* (Grand Rapids: Wm. B. Eerdmans, 1960), pp. 148–75. Cf. Paulus Scharpff, *History of Evangelism*, trans. Helga Bender Henry (Grand Rapids: Wm. B. Eerdmans, 1966), pp. 70–79.

[6] Ibid., p. 15.

[7] Scharpff, *History of Evangelism*, p. 71.

[8] Wesley was so committed to mobilizing every believer as a pacesetter-worker for Christ that at one point he "used the help of more than a dozen different categories of workers to prepare, build, and care for these societies" (Scharpff, *History of Evangelism*, pp. 78–79).

days a week—and used the cell ministry to renew their life strength so that they could witness aggressively at the end of the day, do good deeds for people even poorer than themselves, meet once a week for a long "class" gathering, and for some, pray all night once a month for revival and missions.

It makes one wonder if our contemporary tiredness as individual Christians is not tied to our spiritual depletion, an emptiness related to self-pity, misuse of our tongues, and willful pursuit of self-realization rather than seeking Christ and His missionary will. I think that if he were around today, Wesley would add that we are weak in the spirit of worship and in the assurance of God's love that derives from a self-conscious discipleship built on a clear knowledge of justification by faith.

CORE ELEMENTS IN SMALL GROUPS

I have found a great deal of theological treasure in Wesley's development of small groups. Essentially Wesley saw that his "classes" needed to have three core elements, which our work with small groups at New Life Church has also proved to be crucial for effective outreach. They are as follows:

1. *Spiritual healing and release.* Wesley saturated the class meeting with songs and worship, teaching, testimonies, and exhortation related to justification by faith. He wanted to foster in each believer a strong assurance of God's love, a consciousness of sins forgiven, and the freedom that follows for work and witness. In this faith-building setting he required that all members confess their sins weekly and practice tongue control, expressing itself in praise and strict avoidance of gossip.

2. *Worker mobilization.*[9] Wesley taught the members of his class meetings that they did not exist for their own welfare but for Christ's service. Yet his priority seemed to fall, not on the believer's gifts, but on the kinds of work needing to be done. Each believer was expected to be a deacon to the poor, a

---

[9] Wesley's need of worker-leaders was endless, since each class meeting was to subdivide upon reaching a certain size.

witness to the unconverted, and a prayer warrior. Within this concept of team service, specific gifts were mobilized for teaching, preaching, exhorting, giving, witnessing. These were identified as things needing to be done. Identifying gifts was never done in the abstract.

3. *Outreach action.* What controlled all the aspects of the class and society meetings was the goal of outreach to the lost. Wesley had the people in the groups involved in social action, Bible study, worship, and fellowship, but the center piece was bringing praise to God through focusing the whole undertaking on reaching the lost. Hell was a dreadful reality for Wesley, and he had no intention of merely fattening up poor sinners for hell through social renewal. For instance, a meeting of the class might be devoted to writing letters to non-Christian friends and acquaintances. Believers would gather for the evening and after prayer and worship write evangelistic letters of testimony.

Using a small-group approach such as Wesley's should not be construed as a lack of courage for a pastor to stand on his own two feet. I see it this way: I am a pastor engaged in what is often a lonely battle against immensely powerful forces, both demonic and earthly. In light of this struggle, I have found it heartening to look across the years and see that Wesley had a similar conflict and that he made much progress in it by fastening on to a few key principles and then hanging onto them no matter what. So he has helped me define and sharpen what I had already pretty much learned from my study of the Scriptures and the crucible of pastoral work.

Wesley also inspires my faith by his courage, his willingness to take a stand where he was likely to run into opposition from both inside and outside the church. I believe it was not easy for him and Whitefield to challenge the notion of the church member as a passive survivor, substituting for it the more biblical concept of every believer as a warrior-worker.

Against this background, I now wish to set forth my own view of the nature and function of small groups. These are concepts that I like to believe can be used effectively in any small group of whatever size. My point is that these proposals are not just some "good things to do," but issues of life and death for the ministry of the small group and the church of which it is a part.

THE SMALL-GROUP MODEL

So these final core issues are offered with the hope that you as a pastor or other church leader will banner them forth in your own place and situation. You will find that these concerns have a unique relevance for growth by groups and that they also apply across the board to virtually every ministry in the local church.

1. *The growth model.* Every small group should be led by leaders committed to growth in numbers, including both the assimilation of new members to the church and the reaching of the lost by evangelism. I would suggest a guideline such as this, that the group be organized with a minimum of ten members and plan to divide when its membership reaches twenty-five.

The growth group has two kinds of people: members who are committed to Christ and the goals of the small group, and attenders who are welcomed to the group but either are not yet Christians or are Christians not yet ready for full commitment. Each small group has a leader and an assistant, whom the leader is training for the next small group issuing from this one.

The value of this model is the sanctifying effect of its commitment to growth. The best kind of nurture is given to believers when they are being stretched to do what seems beyond their capabilities. In my experience, groups that have fallen into trouble invariably had neither a plan for growth in numbers nor active evangelism. The alternative to the growth model seems to me to be the Dead Sea model, with believers constantly drinking in truth but stagnating because they are not pouring it out to others.

This growth-by-groups model makes the multiplication of workers almost inevitable. If a group is going to divide fairly soon, then the tasks currently being fulfilled are going to be doubled. Drawing more workers into the ministry overcomes the tendency of Christians to adopt a "rear-echelon" mentality. Everybody is in the fight, and it is hard to gossip and complain if we are busy serving Christ. Holiness is an active virtue and must not be allowed to rust through sitting on the sidelines.

2. *The healing model.* Many believers coming into a small group are not yet ready for active witnessing. Some may be emotionally crippled—perhaps bitter and angry toward a spouse who has just left or deeply resentful in attitude toward parents or other authority figures. Others may be overwhelmed by the intensity of sexual temptation or job-related problems. That is why the small group must provide pastoral care. But this pastoral care must be more than just counseling. In fact, many people with intense problems have been overcounseled, with little evidence of growth and benefit resulting from it.

Instead, what is needed is to build faith by saturating the mind with the gospel of grace, so that lives can be built on the presupposition of Christ's atonement and His present availability as a living, loving Lord.

David Powlison, counselor and theoretician for the Christian Counseling and Educational Foundation, recently told me, "I'm beginning to think that many counseling crises exist only because people do not know how to get in touch with Jesus as a living Lord." He said he has gradually shifted his whole counseling method so that the central focus is on the gospel itself as the cleansing and healing power of God. Translated into small-group ministry, this means we need only to establish two things to see people released from their bondage for service: one is the reality of justification by faith, and the other is the reality of Christ's present rule over our lives by faith.

This is what needs to be brought into every dimension of the small groups. We could begin in our groups by emphasizing the learning of the verses of Charles Wesley's great hymn on the gospel and grace, "And Can It Be?" Then we could sing it until it had turned into living faith and the thoroughgoing conviction that all our sins are fully removed. We could also have the groups read Horatius Bonar's *Peace with God* or Spurgeon's *All of Grace* or my pamphlet "Forgiven." A study of Romans or Galatians would also be helpful.

Within that framework we can begin to work on tongue control. This is the logical next step in the pattern delineated in this book. The basic thought is that God through the gospel no longer condemns us, and therefore we are no longer to condemn others either with suspicious, judging attitudes or by slanderous, gossiping tongues. Instead, we commit ourselves to strive together to shift from slander and backbiting to praising God, affirming one another, and witnessing to non-Christians about Christ.

In small groups we have an opportunity to help people at close range to stop wounding their consciences by complaining about and sniping at others. In the small groups at New Life Church in late 1974 and early 1975, Elder Dan Herron and Deacon James Trott organized the first small group and placed major stress on tongue control. Dan taught that each believer was expected never again to say something negative or hurtful about another person but rather, if there were conflicts, the offended person was to go directly to the offender and follow the pattern of discipline described in Matthew 18:15–17.

I am convinced that these beginning efforts toward godly obedience were pleasing to God and unleashed the Holy Spirit on the church in a new way. The result was that the quality of discipleship greatly improved and within a year or so, about one hundred new people showed up at our church.

3. *The worker model.* I once heard the pastor of a large church tell how a woman came to him with a host of problems that were bringing her near to a nervous breakdown. After hearing her story, the pastor thought for a minute and wrote down a name and address. He handed the paper to the woman and said, "This lady has all your problems and is also very poor. So go bake her a cake and take it to her and tell her that Jesus loves her. The minute you do that, you'll feel a lot better about yourself."

The woman did as she was asked and returned to the pastor's office the next day. She said, "When I took the cake into that poor woman's room I began to forget my problems as I tried to help her with hers."

It may not always be quite that simple to mobilize believers for Christ's kingdom work, but it almost is. Once we have saturated people with the gospel in song, testimony, preaching, and teaching, we ought to expect them to be able to serve others and to find increased liberation in that service.

To prepare believers for becoming workers serving Christ, I use a book by John White, *The Cost of Commitment*, because it deals effectively with the hangups and fears that dog Christian workers. After they have studied this book, I challenge the members of the group to think of themselves as deacons called of Christ to aim for complete obedience to Him. I follow this with specific assignments such as adopting a new member of the group as a personal friend, raking leaves for an elderly person living down the street from the group's meeting place, providing refreshments for the group once a month, or painting the room of a shut-in who lacks the strength to do it. In case of sickness, everyone is expected to contribute hot meals.

Then, within the context of what needs to be done, I seek out and prepare people to exercise the following gifts in the group: leader, assistant leader, deacons, worship leader, musicians, hospitality leader, children's leaders, Bible teachers, and exhorter—a role that entails encouraging the group and admonishing individuals for sins. For example, the hospitality leader would be responsible for calling people who miss the meetings and for making sure that visitors to the church service have a direct invitation to come to the group and are welcomed into it. We might expect to find as many as eight or ten gifts being exercised in a meeting on any given evening.

4. *The missionary model.* Small groups are ideal for outreach. They form natural teams for evangelism if they are properly prepared and understand how to do this work.

Preparation is essential, because many people get almost tongue-tied when it comes to witnessing. I believe a fundamental reason for this is a lack of fellowship with the Father. You can hardly talk about the wonder of His love in Christ if you don't really think He likes you very much and prayer is alien to you. So all of us need ongoing release from acting like orphans living without a Father and without the empowerment of His Spirit of love.

The key issue here is often as simple and old-fashioned as

learning how to confess our sins. This is an essential practice if we are to be freed for witness, speaking the truth with humble joy and self-forgetting kindness. This brings to mind Wesley's seemingly legalistic requirement of a weekly confession of sins by everyone in the class meeting. Though I do not think this should be legalistically required, I believe that one role of the leaders is regularly to confess their sins and weaknesses to the group. When this is done with both discretion and frankness, it can work wonders to open up people to tell the real truth about themselves to others. In my experience, whenever a group leader opens up, other members follow suit. It becomes a cleansing, healing preparation for missionary endeavor and takes the legalism out of the whole picture by restoring to members the joy of salvation.[10]

EQUIPPED FOR OUTREACH

How can a small group engage in effective evangelistic outreach without attempting something that is beyond its grasp or inappropriate to the person targeted?

One wrong way to do it is to do what we once planned for our neighbors. We invited them to a "hospitality evening." Unfortunately, some of the leaders did not understand the idea of a low-key approach and wanted everything "out in the open." So we found ourselves beginning with Scripture songs and hymns, followed by prayer, and some in-group discussion. By the time we got to the hospitality we had stamped "religious" over the whole evening. That was overkill, and it suggested to us that our group needed training in the kind of patient, natural evangelism that characterized Jesus' approach to the woman at the well (John 4).

Next time, a different strategy will be used. For Christmas, two of our members—a medical doctor and his wife—will invite their neighbors to a carol sing. It will be made clear in the invitation that the members of the Christian small group

---

[10] As John White has pointed out in his book, *Healing the Wounded: The Costly Love of Church Discipline* (Downers Grove, Ill.: InterVarsity, 1985), the confession of sins needs to be both vertical to God and horizontal to man. He says, "The practice of confessing our sins to one another can make the Godward transaction more real" (p. 183).

will be hosting them. But it will be just that, a carol sing, with a word of greeting from the host describing the small group and explaining its purpose. Any direct witnessing will occur only through individual conversations. Making friends is a crucial first step for this kind of group outreach.

Similarly, one of our small groups in a rural area wanted to have an evangelistic picnic in the group leader's backyard. I urged them not to have singing and praying but only hospitality and entertainment provided by the church's team of Christian clowns. This would be followed by the host giving his testimony to the neighbors, many of whom already knew him well and were ready to hear what he had to say.

Small groups can be organized solely to reach a particular group in the community such as international students, medical people, or residents of a nursing home. We have had numerous groups of this kind in our church and found that the clear missionary direction of the group served to heighten oneness and fellowship among the believers. It is usually expected that Christian medical people are the ones most qualified to reach their peers. So from the start such a group should be oriented around commitments made by Christian medical personnel who are willing to seek out and invite to meetings non-Christians who can be attracted by relevant subjects for discussion or a special speaker.

It is also possible to invite non-Christian guests to a regular meeting of the small group if they are carefully selected and the evening features a meal. But usually such invitations are most effective when the non-Christian guest has already shown an interest in Christianity, as by attending a Bible study or attending church services. In these cases, inviting the non-Christian can be a very effective way of witnessing, since they are enabled to gain an "inside" look at the life of Christians and get a taste of Christian fellowship.

So let us go forward with this vision. Let us give it no rest until we see more and more people in our churches changing from merely surviving to working for Christ, becoming His soldiers in the noblest cause this world has ever seen.

ACTION STEPS

1. Read the chapter, "Association for Communication," in Carl Wilson's book, *With Christ in the School of Disciple Building* (pp. 171–83).
2. Spend the next six months to a year developing in your congregation what Wilson calls "casual association for repentance and faith." Use the means of small, informal, social gatherings emphasizing friendship leading to shared repentance and faith. For instruction and discussion consider either John White's *Cost of Commitment* or my *Repentance and Twentieth Century Man.*
3. List the names of ten people you have been "casually associating with"—teachable Christians who you think would make up a well-balanced small group. Include in your list a potential leader, an assistant leader, five believers who look more like pacesetters than survivors, and three believers who are just surviving.
4. Have the people in the list above read this chapter and gather to discuss it. After discussion, organize those who respond into a growth group. After one year's growth, spin off a second group that has approximately the same makeup as the original group.

READING SHELF

ARN, WIN. *How to Effectively Incorporate New Members.* Pasadena: Institute for American Church Growth, n.d.

COLEMAN, LYMAN. *Body Building.* Nashville: Abingdon, 1981.

COLEMAN, ROBERT. *The Master Plan of Evangelism.* Westwood, N.J.: Fleming H. Revell, 1964.

EIMS, LeROY. *The Lost Art of Disciple Making.* Grand Rapids: Zondervan, 1978.

Flocks, Shepherd's Guide, Leadership Training Guide. Panorama City, Calif.: Grace Community Church, 1985.

GRIFFIN, EM. *Getting Together: A Guide for Good Groups.* Downers Grove, Ill.: InterVarsity, 1982.

Small Group Leaders' Handbook. Downers Grove, Ill.: InterVarsity, 1982. (Contributing authors include Steve Barker, Judy Johnson, Jimmy Long, Rob Malone, and Ron Nicholas.)

VERSTRATEN, CHARLES A. *How to Start Lay Shepherding Ministries.* Grand Rapids: Baker, 1983.

WILSON, CARL. *With Christ in the School of Disciple Building.* Grand Rapids: Zondervan, 1976.

EPILOGUE:
Risk or Rust

As a leader you may respond to this book by saying, "My personality is so different from the author's that some things just would not work for me." Or you may reason, "Some of the things done at New Life Church simply would not fit in our congregation." Let's acknowledge the personality differences and the uniqueness of our churches. Nonetheless, the core issues we have discussed should fit into the renewal and outreach of any local church. Their elements can be adapted to many different circumstances of congregational life.

The key question is, Do you have the courage of faith to think through the issues—to discern God's will for your congregation?

My concern is that recognizing the risks may keep you from doing anything about the ingrown church. But I believe that discerning risk-taking is essential to the healthy growth of church leaders and congregations. As leaders and members of churches we are continually faced with a choice: either take risks or rust where we are. By risk-taking I mean a willingness to assess the kind of ideas that are presented in this book and to use them in church life, with the knowledge that doing so makes us vulnerable to personal hurt.

Often, I believe, our problem as leaders is that we have unconsciously chosen to rust where we are, because of the fear of failing or of losing our dignity. When this happens, the armor of the Christian warrior oxidizes at the joints so that forward movement is virtually impossible until the underlying love of self is renounced. I believe that God's grace sought in humility will enable us to renounce our fears and the love of preeminence that often lies behind them. He gives grace to the humble that includes a healthy self-fulfillment in Christ, a sanity of mind consisting largely of a certain good-humored carelessness about our honor and reputation.

We need to accept the reality that every ministry that is from God will have some failures in it. We must make the mistakes that go with maturing or we cannot become an effective leader in Christ's sheepfold. We must be willing to take a risk every time we preach a sermon with daring and specific applications. When we organize evangelism we may take missteps that could give opportunity to critics to have their say. Try doing diaconal work and we may discover as we build the program how little care many people have for the poor and the sick. Perhaps for a time the work will melt away. So be it, but persevere. As we persevere, we will find that we are being helped by the Spirit not to repeat the same old mistakes; we will discover that God-sized successes are beginning to come. But it would never have happened if we were not willing at some point to learn the ropes by plunging in where we lacked the ability and experience.

This doesn't mean that there is no foolish risk-taking or action steps that were motivated more by presumption than by faith. I am persuaded that a primary problem of many pastors is that they never had a solid program of ministry preparation under the guidance of an older pastor. Yet God can bless even that major misstep. I know I needed more pastoral training before I became a pastor. But God used this to bring me to knowledge of Himself and the power of the gospel.

I suspect that without being out there all by myself, I would never have stumbled onto the power of the gospel and the empowerment for ministry that is born out of desperate prayer.

So, fellow pacesetter, go to the work with hope, for we have a big God with abundant grace who has given us a message that can change the hardest human heart.